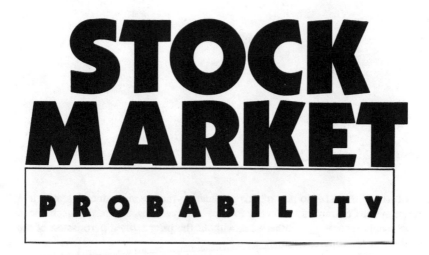

STOCK MARKET

PROBABILITY

How to Improve
the Odds of Making
Better
Investment Decisions

Joseph E. Murphy, Jr.

Probus Publishing Company
Chicago, Illinois

Library of Congress Cataloging-in-Publication Data Available

ISBN: 1-55738-017-1

Printed in the United States of America

1   2   3   4   5   6   7   8   9   0

To Diana, Michael, and John

Contents

V

Preface

This book describes specific new techniques to estimate probabilities of future events that will affect investments. Some techniques can be applied to searching for solutions on mutual funds, others applied to determinations on individual stocks; some aid in market timing, and others aid in estimating probabilities of future profit and loss.

The premise of this book, given the fact that the precise future of any investment is unknown, is that it nevertheless is often possible to make calculated estimates of the alternative probabilities of various outcomes. The end product is a probability statement which will describe the distributions of returns on a stock or the entire market, and the distribution of future interest rates or of future earnings or dividends. By making these probability distributions, as developed in this book, it is possible to make sharper and better qualified decisions and thereby improve investment returns.

Although these techniques are based on well-established statistical methodology, many of the specific concepts and calculations as applied to investments are unique to this book. This is so because they are based on a perspective not normally taught in the business schools or practiced on Wall Street.

But learning these new techniques, and applying them to your own investment problems or those of your customers, enables you to better manage your investment risk and improve your investment returns. Also, you may see the market from quite a different viewpoint than you held before.

Acknowledgments

The foundation for my understanding of the stock market came from Maury Osborne, with whom I've been privileged to work for nearly a decade.

I am also indebted to Marlin Bree, for editorial suggestions and assistance, and to Jim Harris, Dick Schall, Dennis Senneseth for reading the manuscript and making suggestions and corrections. J. Michael Jeffers of Probus helped me restructure the book.

                                                                    Joseph E. Murphy

CHAPTER 1

Overview

Stock prices and corporate financial variables have certain fundamental characteristics which may be used to derive estimates of the future. These estimates can be applied to evaluate investment decisions and to refine corporate financial policy. The fundamental characteristics form the basis for deriving rules about which kinds of estimates can be made, and which cannot.

The Random Walk

The most fundamental feature of stock prices, corporate sales, and earnings is that differences in the logs of these variables resemble approximately a random walk. While a random walk—typified by a drunk wandering over a plain—would seem to defy all estimates of the future, it nevertheless obeys two major characteristics which can be studied and used.

The first characteristic of a random walk is that the distribution of changes in (the logs of) a variable like stock prices, or corporate earnings or revenues, conforms to an approximately normal distribution.

The normal distribution, the most common distribution in the world, is well known and has been extensively studied. We can use the normal distribution to estimate the probability of a future change of any magnitude. This application of the normal distribution gives us an approximate and very powerful tool for making estimates about the future.

The second characteristic is that the dispersion of the distribution of a random variable, measured by the standard deviation, rises with the square root of the holding period, or time.

This square root of time rule is true of stock prices, earnings, and other financial variables. The rule applies in two ways: 1) to the dispersion of a single series, like the price of IBM; and 2) to the cross-section dispersion, or the dispersion across stocks. Cross-section dispersion is like the dispersion

3

of particles of smoke emerging from a chimney: the particles gradually disperse or spread out in the sky.

We can use the second characteristic, the square root of time rule, to estimate probabilities over any time or holding interval. By measuring the standard deviation of the series we are interested in and then combining the normal distribution and the square root of time rule, we can make probability estimates about the future.

We can make future estimates for such things as returns on a single stock, returns on mutual funds, future earnings and dividends, or the probability of loss. The estimates are probability statements like the following: the probability of a 20-percent return on this stock is only 1 in 20, or the probability of a 30-percent decline in earnings is 1 in 40. We can prepare a distribution of various outcomes and their probabilities.

Chapters 10–14 are devoted to demonstrating how to make probability estimates and how to use them.

Characteristics of Randomness

The lognormal distribution and the rise in cross section dispersion over time have two further characteristics.

One characteristic is the presence of an upward bias to a random series like the stock market, a long-term trend which can be computed from the standard deviation. Although this important feature was pointed out many years ago, it has been entirely neglected.

The other characteristic is that for any equally weighted portfolio, we can estimate the future distribution of assets after any holding period. The same estimate can be made for the rankings of companies by sales, profits, or market values.

These two characteristics of randomness, the trend and the terminal distribution, give us a view from above, a large scale map, of what is taking place in the stock market and the corporate world. It tells us what will happen to our stock portfolios if we do not make changes, and what our industry is likely to look like after the passage of time. These topics are covered in Chapters 15–17.

Rules of Probability

Just as the stock market may be a place for legalized gambling, like the race track, the behavior of market prices, earnings, revenues, and other financial variables exhibit some features of the race.

At the start of the race, all the horses are even. Halfway down the track one or more take the lead, and a larger group of horses lag behind. As the race continues, the spread between the horses, the dispersion, widens. At midpoint, the probability that the last horse will surpass the first is low, yet the probability that the last will begin to catch up may be even.

Exactly the same thing happens in the stock market. The largest company is likely to remain the largest; the company with the biggest share of market is likely to retain it; and the company with the highest return on equity is likely to continue to earn the highest return.

But if stock prices and corporate earnings are approximately random, as they seem to be, then relative growth in one period will not bear any systematic relationship to relative growth in another. Size, share of market, return on equity, or past performance are likely to bear little relation to future growth. That means last year's best mutual fund or stock, has only an even chance of doing better than average next year.

The above relationships may be derived from the underlying characteristics of random processes, like stock price changes, and stated in terms of rules or laws. The rules suggest that it is very difficult to make a precise prediction, though it is quite possible to make probability estimates. Chapter 21 describes the rules, or laws, and how to apply them. The rules also suggest that many common practices and beliefs are without merit.

CHAPTER 2

The Standard Deviation, the Normal Distribution, and Natural Logarithms—Concepts Useful to Studying the Stock Market

To describe the stock market, we need concepts that adequately describe uncertainty, indeterminacy, or, if you prefer, the chaos of highly variant data. There are three concepts used throughout this book which we will define at the outset—the standard deviation, the normal distribution, and natural logarithm.

The first two concepts are useful in describing indeterminant, or highly variably, data. The last is used to homogenize data covering long periods in calculating the standard deviation and preparing tables of distributions. (Readers who are familiar with these concepts can proceed to the next chapter.)

The Standard Deviation

The standard deviation is a measure of the spread or dispersion of a set of numbers. It is defined as the square root of the variance with the variance defined in the following way:

Variance = Sum (Value − Average Value)^2/Number of Values   *divided by the # of values*

The variance is the sum of the squares of deviations from the mean, as defined above. Since the square of a number is always positive, the variance is always positive even though many of the values will be negative.

The standard deviation is the square root of the variance. It is defined as

Standard Deviation = Variance$^{.5}$

We can compute the standard deviation of annual returns on the Standard & Poor's 500 Stock Index as follows:

Table 2.1 Computation of Standard Deviation

Year	Annual Return %	Annual _ Average Return Return	$\left(\dfrac{Annual}{Return} \_ \dfrac{Average}{Return}\right)^2$
1977	−11.5	−15.4	236.6
1978	1.1	− 2.8	7.9
1979	−12.3	8.4	71.1
1980	25.8	21.9	479.3
1981	− 9.7	−13.6	185.2
1982	14.8	10.9	118.4
1983	17.3	13.4	179.3
1984	1.4	− 2.5	6.1
1985	26.3	22.4	504.2

Average return   3.9%

Sum of squared deviations   1788.2

Average of sum of squared deviations gives
    variance (1788.2/9)   198.7

Square root of variance gives standard deviation $(198.7)^{.5}$ 18.3%

As can be seen, returns on the S&P 500 vary from year to year. The mean annual return was 3.9 percent and the standard deviation was 18.3 percent. Usually two thirds of the returns will fall within one standard deviation of the mean. The range of one standard deviation of the mean for the above data is −14.4 percent to +22.2 percent. Seven of the nine returns do fall within one standard deviation of the mean value.

The Normal Distribution

A distribution is a classification of values by range. Examples are the distribution of stock prices, and the distribution of yields on stocks. At any given time there are so many stocks with a 1–1.9-percent yield, so many with a 2–2.9-percent yield, and so on up to perhaps a given number of stocks with a 10 –10.9-percent yield. A table giving the number of stocks in each yield range is called a table of the distribution of yields, or a distribution of yields. The distribution, or the frequency distribution, is used to classify the values in an easy, shorthand way.

A normal distribution is bell-shaped and symmetrical. The height and width of its curve is determined by the standard deviation. If the standard deviation is small, the distribution will be tall and thin. If the standard deviation is large, the distribution will be short and wide.

Both kinds are normal. For all normal distributions, 68 percent of the values lie within 1 standard deviation of the mean; 95 percent of the values lie within two standard deviations of the mean.   18% within 3

If we know the standard deviation, we can state precisely what proportion of the values lie above or below any standard deviation from the mean, or, even more useful, within any two standard deviations. Figure 2.1 shows a normal distribution.

The area of the curve represents the proportion of values which lie within. Two-thirds of the area lies within one standard deviation of the mean; ninety-five percent of the area lies within two standard deviations of the mean. Using a table for the normal distribution, we can calculate the proportion of values that fall within any range of standard deviations.

Stock returns, as defined below, are approximately normal. Consequently we can determine the distribution of historical returns over any period, compute the standard deviation, and fit that distribution to the normal curve. The normal distribution can then be applied to estimating the probability distribution of future stock returns.

Natural Logarithms

The degree of change in a stock price series tends to be proportional to the level of the series; that in turn makes changes in the series highly dependent on the price level. If we express the prices in terms of their natural logarithms, we obtain a new series in which variation in the series is not dependent on the level. The series is homogenized, so to speak, like an egg after it has been beaten up.

Natural logarithms are also useful for computing rates of return using continuous compounding. For returns of from 1 percent to 15 percent, the log change is close to the percent change. This near-equivalence is demonstrated by the following illustration.

The rate of return on a stock not paying dividends is defined as:

Return = (Ending Price − Beginning Price)/Beginning Price

Normally the return is expressed in percent, which is accomplished by multiplying the result of the above equation by 100.

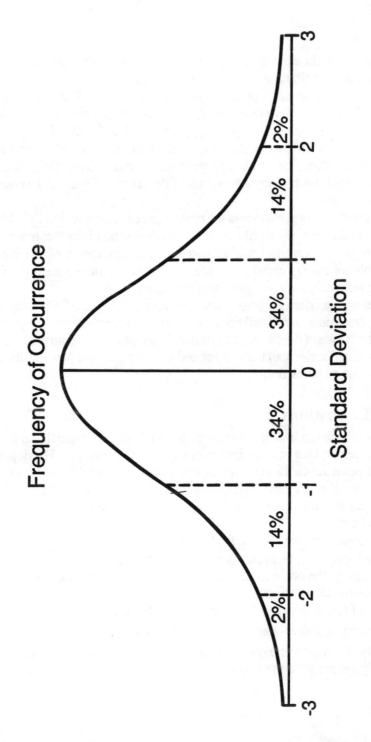

Figure 2.1 The Normal Curve

Using $1.10 as the ending price and $1.00 as the beginning price, we calculate the rate of return as:

Return = (1.10 – 1.00)/1.00

= 0.10

To express 0.10 in percent, we multiply 0.10 by 100 and obtain a return of 10 percent.

We can perform the same calculation in natural logarithms, with only a slight modification.

Return = Nat. Log(Ending Price) – Nat. Log(Beg. Price)

= Nat. Log(1.10) – Nat. Log(1.00)

= 0.10 – 0.00

= 0.10

Taking the differences in successive items in a price series can be called taking first differences. If we take the log differences in a series of monthly prices of a stock, we obtain a series of monthly rates of return based on price and excluding dividend.

The natural logarithm has several advantages:

1. First differences in the natural logs of prices are rates of return.

2. The data is homogenized since the differences no longer depend on the level of prices.

3. The distribution of first differences in the logs of price, and therefore of rates of return, is more approximately normal than first differences in the original prices.

Examples of natural logs are shown in Table 2.2.

Table 2.2 Examples of Natural Logarithms

Number	Natural Logarithm
0.85	–0.16
0.90	–0.11
1.00	0.00
1.05	0.05
1.10	0.10
1.15	0.14
1.20	0.18

It is useful to know that the following two expressions are equivalent:

Nat. Log(Ending Price) – Nat. Log(Beginning Price)

$\qquad$ = Nat. Log(Ending Price/Beginning Price)

◆ ◆ ◆

The standard deviation can be used to measure the variability of a set of numbers. The standard deviation determines the shape of normal curve and the normal curve approximates first differences in the natural logarithms of stock prices. By using the three measures—the standard deviation, the normal curve, and natural logarithms—we will be able to derive probability estimates of the future.

CHAPTER 3

The Statistical Basis for Estimating Future Probable Changes in Stock Prices

If you know that the distribution of changes in a series is normal and if you know the standard deviation, you can make probability estimates of the future. Though the distribution of stock price changes is not normal, we still can perform transformations to make it approximately normal.

The standard deviation for stock prices rises in a regular way so that if we know its value for one time interval, we can compute it for any other time interval.

Figure 3.1 graphs the monthly closing price of the S&P 500 from 1883 to 1985. This index combines the Cowles Common Stock index and the S&P 500 which began in 1938.

There are some significant features of this figure. First, the index rose substantially over the period. In 1883 the index was 5.34 and by the end of 1985 it had reached 166.4. While that seems like a substantial rise, it represents an average annual compound growth of only 3.4 percent. Second, the series exhibits considerable fluctuation. The degree of fluctuation appears to be much greater in the latter part of the period, on the right of the figure.

We can actually examine the degree of fluctuation in greater detail by plotting the monthly changes in the index instead of the index itself. Figure 3.2 shows the monthly change in price, beginning in 1883 and ending in 1985. Each bar on the figure shows the dollar rise or fall in price during the month.

Some significant features emerge from this figure also. Increases and decreases in the index occur regularly throughout the period, more or less at random. Scanning the figure, it is very difficult to ascertain whether the next change would be up or down. There is a lot of chaos in the data.

There also seem to be nearly as many decreases as increases. In fact, there are more decreases than increases, 54 percent versus 46 percent. Another significant feature is that the degree of fluctuation appears to be much higher in the latter part of the period, when price of the S&P 500 was much higher.

17

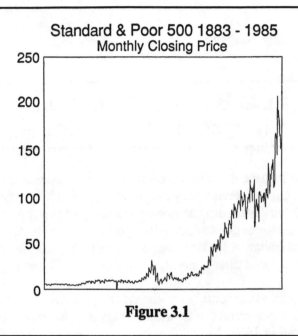

Figure 3.1

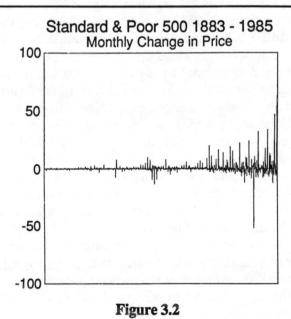

Figure 3.2

The fact that the degree of fluctuation was much higher at high levels of the index suggests that the degree of change in the index may be proportional to the level of the index.

In other words, the probability of a $1 change when the index was $10 might be the same as the probability of a $10 change when the index was $100. Since this seems to be the case, any estimate of the degree of change must depend on the level of the index.

We need some way to remove the influence of the effect of the level of the index on the degree of change. One way is to convert to logarithms. Figure 3.3 shows the same index, the S&P 500, using the natural logarithms of the index instead of the original index. The figure shows how the influence of the level of rates was removed.

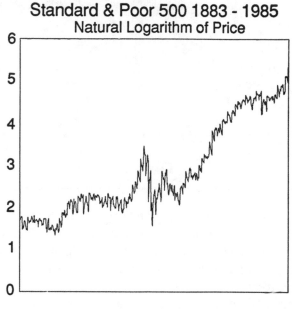

Figure 3.3

As can be seen, the sharp difference between the initial and final values has disappeared. The index still rises, but the degree of fluctuation appears to be more even throughout, as we would expect from a log transformation. Changes, or first differences, in the logarithms are even more accurate than the logarithms themselves. The next figure, Figure 3.4, shows monthly changes in the natural logarithms of the S&P 500 Index. It is the same kind of figure as the price difference figure, but now it is based on the logarithms.

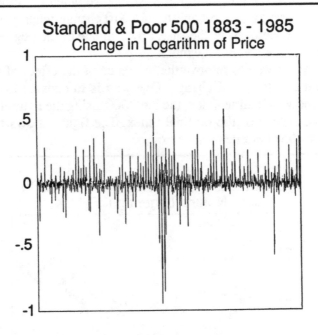

Figure 3.4

Figure 3.4 reveals a very striking and important point. There is no longer any trend in the degree of fluctuation in the S&P 500 Index. The conversion to natural logarithms has removed the effect of the level of price on the degree of fluctuation. The monthly differences in the logs of price shown in Figure 3.4 are roughly the same over the entire span of years 1883–1985. The significant point of this figure is that in studying fluctuations in stock prices, we should homogenize the data by taking the logs of the original prices. By so doing, we eliminate the effect on fluctuation caused by the particular level of the index.

In homogenizing the data we used the natural logarithms of the index instead of the index itself. The first differences in the logs were equally volatile throughout the entire century.

◆ ◆ ◆

For random series, the standard deviation rises with the square root of the difference interval, or holding period. In Figure 3.3 we graphed changes in the S&P 500 over 1-month intervals. We can compute the standard deviation of the 1-month changes as a measure of the monthly volatility. This will give us a single number for 1-month volatility—the 1-month standard deviation. We can also take 2-month changes and compute the standard deviation. In fact, we can compute the standard deviation for a variety of intervals, 1-month, 2-month, 3-month—even 100-month changes.

For a purely random series, the standard deviation will rise with the square root of the differencing interval—in this case the number of months. That means that we will get a series like that shown in Table 3.1.

Table 3.1 Standard Deviation of a Random Series

Interval in Months	Standard Deviation s
1	1 × s
2	1.41 × s
3	1.73 × s
4	2 × s
9	3 × s
16	4 × s
25	5 × s

For common stock prices, the standard deviation does increase approximately with the square root of the differencing interval, or holding period. Figure 3.5 shows that relationship for the standard deviation of changes in the logs of the S&P 500 Index from 1883 to 1985.

In Figure 3.5, the standard deviation rises with increases in the difference interval (the number of months). The relationship is not perfect, but it approximates the square root rule. The slope is not quite 0.5, the square root value, but 0.42, and the relationship is highly significant with a coefficient of correlation of 0.97. We can use this relationship to estimate the distribution of price changes for any time interval, from one day to five to ten years, once we know that the distribution is approximately normal.

Figure 3.6 is a histogram of the distribution of monthly changes in the logs of the S&P 500. The distribution is bell-shaped, high at the center, and thin

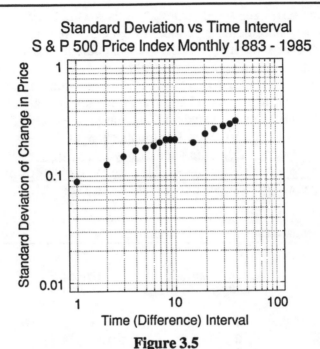

Figure 3.5

with wide tails. It is only approximately normal, but sufficiently so that we can use the normal distribution to make probability estimates of the future.

Summary

Several important matters have been addressed in this chapter.

For a major stock price index you can homogenize the data by taking first differences in the natural logarithms of price. In so doing, you obtain a measure of volatility that does not depend on how high the index is, or how low, or what historical period you pick. There are some exceptions, of course, such as the aberrations of 1929 or 1987.

For a stock price series, the measure of volatility, the standard deviation, rises roughly with the square root of the holding period, or time. The square root of time relationship makes it possible to estimate the standard deviation for any length period, provided you know it for one period. If the distribution is normal and we know the standard deviation, we can calculate prob-

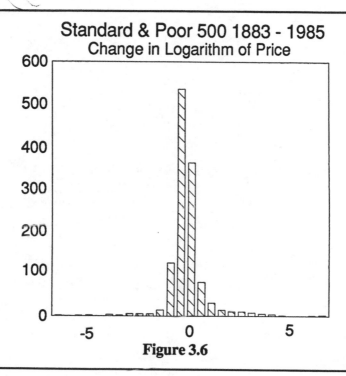

Standard & Poor 500 1883 - 1985
Change in Logarithm of Price

Figure 3.6

able changes. The distribution of changes in the logs of price is bell-shaped and approximately normal.

We have just described the foundation for the method of estimating probable changes in the prices of the stock market. The same method will work for many other economic series, from company revenues to company profit and loss.

CHAPTER 4

How Knowing the Probability Can Improve Your Investment Decisions

If one could predict a specific event, such as how high the price of Crypton will go next week or how low profit margins will fall next year, one could become very rich. Unfortunately, no-one's financial crystal ball is enough in focus to make accurate predictions. Even though we can't predict the specific, we can do the next best thing: predict the probability, because changes in stock prices and other financial variables, though thoroughly chaotic, are nevertheless distributed surprisingly well according to the laws of probability.

Knowing the probability, then, can be very helpful in a wide range of problems. Its usefulness is illustrated in the following investment situation examples. Later on we will discuss how to estimate probabilities to help solve your specific investment situations more profitably.

Investment Problem 1

Whether to Buy a Bond Now—or Wait

John Ames had money to invest. He wanted to buy long term bonds because he wouldn't need the money for ten years. But he wanted and needed the income. Rates on 10-year bonds were 8 percent. Seeking advice, he was told that rates would rise to 10 percent within the next year, and to wait until they did before buying long bonds.

John did some hard thinking. "If that is absolutely true, with a 100-percent probability of an increase, then I should wait. But if the advice was not very certain, then I should not wait," thought John. He wanted more certainty, so he asked another adviser how likely it was that rates would reach 10 percent. "The probability is very low," he was told. "Only 3 percent. And there's an equal probability that rates could drop to 6.4 percent"

Knowing that there is a probability of only 3 percent that 10-year bond rates will rise to 10 percent was enough for John. He decided that the odds were too low. He also didn't want to be faced with lower rates. So he bought the 10-year bonds.

Knowing the probability that rates would rise a given amount enabled John to make an informed decision on bond investment.

Investment Problem 2
How to Estimate Whether a Firm Will Be Profitable

Having sold his company, Dick Jensen wanted to buy another. After a long search, he had narrowed his choice to Crick Electronics, and one other. Crick had an exciting product, served a growing industry—and was cheap.

There was only one problem. The firm had lost money in two of the past five years. Dick did not want to have a problem company and he was concerned that this one might have losses in the future. He would not want to buy unless he was reasonably sure to profit.

The seller, Mr. Harris, assured him that there would be no future losses. "The odds of a future loss are less than one in a thousand," he affirmed, "since we have corrected the problems."

If Harris was anywhere near right, Dick would buy. But were the odds really one in a thousand?

Dick went to his accountant, who calculated the probability of that firm suffering a future loss. The accountant derived the probability from the standard deviation of past changes in earnings and the current level of earnings.

The accountant's answer was not at all what Dick expected. "The probability of a future loss," said the accountant, "is 40 percent."

Dick initially questioned the calculation, but when he saw how it was done, he accepted the result. With the prospect of that high probability of loss, Dick decided to pass on Crick—he knew now that the low price reflected the risk. He turned to his second choice, which turned out to be a good buy.

Knowing the probability that a firm will lose money in the future can help you decide whether you want to buy or not buy.

Investment Problem 3
How Likely is the Dividend to Be Cut?

Skip Johnson had picked a stock primarily on the basis of its dividend return. Of course, he also was interested in potential price appreciation since Xron was in a growth industry, had a solid niche in the market, and was considered well-managed.

But what especially interested Skip Johnson was the 10-percent dividend yield. Skip's main concern was that the dividend might be cut. When he asked his broker, the answer was prompt. "Of course not, there is less than one chance in a hundred they'll cut the dividend. Don't give it a thought."

Seeking assurance, Skip asked a security analyst what the likelihood was they'd cut the dividend.

He was told the that the probability could be estimated from the payout ratio. Skip listened carefully as the analyst explained the procedure. The probability of a cut surprised him—it was an astounding 70 percent.

"A long way from one in a hundred," he mused to himself. Skip did not buy the stock—but he did get another broker.

Investment Problem 4
The Odds of a Rise in Margins

Jack Kirby wanted to expand his company, Melor Radio, into a new market. Adding a second radio station in a neighboring state would give him much broader coverage. To make the purchase, Kirby had to meet the interest charges. The price of the station seemed too high to do that, unless its profit margins could be raised. Current operating margins on the new station were 20 percent, against a national average of 30 percent. Kirby felt that if he could raise margins to 30 percent, he then could afford to make the purchase at an acceptable price.

Could he increase margins that much? He asked his accountant what the odds were of getting to the higher figure. The accountant determined what costs might be cut to come up with an estimate. After a week of going over the data, he calculated he might get to 30 percent if all possible cuts were made and everything worked out well—including no softening in the local or national markets.

Then check, the accountant estimated the probability of getting to 30 percent by looking at past changes in margins. This was a different method, but it would provide a good check. When he finished, he brought both results to Kirby.

"Based on past changes in margins," he said, "the probability of reaching 30 percent is about one in five—a 20-percent probability."

Kirby pondered for some time, then decided to lower his bid to give himself a greater margin of safety. Frankly, he didn't like the odds—lowering the bid would make it possible to do the deal with lower margins than 30 percent.

The next day his lower bid won. He was glad his accountant had made the probability estimate. He was able to increase margins to the lower target of 26 percent, and pay off the loan.

Investment Problem 5
Which Stock Will Have the Higher Future Yield?

Terry Haynes wanted to know whether five years from now a stock which was yielding 4 percent would have a higher yield, based on today's price and the future dividend, than another stock which was yielding 8 percent. Current wisdom seemed to indicate that the lower yielding stock was in a faster growing company. When he asked a friend in the investment business, he was told that the 4-percent stock would likely have a higher yield in the future, but it might take more than five years. Another friend was more definite.

"Certainly," he said, "the 4-percent yield will be higher."

Not satisfied with this advice, Terry turned to a statistician, who proceeded to calculate the probability. "The probability is only 10 percent," said the statistician, "that the lower yield stock will have a higher yield five years from now. Both yields," he added, "based on present price."

When it was explained to him, Terry saw how the statistician had derived the probability and he accepted it. He wanted the higher income, but he became even more intrigued by the price appreciation prospects of the lower yielding stock. He decided to take a chance on it, even though the income, now and in the future, was probably going to be much lower.

These examples illustrate how knowing the probability can help shape a more informed decision. Later on, we'll discuss how to calculate probability for your own particular investment problem. But first, we must understand some of the main underlying characteristics of stock prices, earnings, and other related things.

CHAPTER 5

The Dispersion of Stock Prices

On a stock trade, it's logical to expect that the price rise anticipated by the buyer equals the price decline anticipated by the seller. Since the opposing views offset each other, the probabilities of a rise or fall in price are equal. For a stock market, like the New York Stock Exchange, where buyers and sellers congregate and trades take place, we can describe the expected change (in the log of price) as:

$$E(\log_e \text{price}) = 0 \tag{1}$$

In this case—and if the trades are independent in a probability sense as they may be expected to be—then we may expect the following: the distribution of changes in the logs of price will be normal, with a mean of zero and a dispersion which increases as the square root of the number of transactions.

If transactions occur evenly through time, as they do on average, then dispersion will increase with the square root of time. Here we measure dispersion by the standard deviation of changes in the logs of price:

$$\text{standard deviation} = \text{standard deviation} \times \text{time}^{.5} \tag{2}$$

The central limit theorem assumes that the distribution of sums of price changes will approach a normal distribution for large numbers of transactions, whatever the distribution of the individual price changes.

The first person to examine the distribution of changes in stock prices was M.F.M. Osborne. Osborne looked at the distribution of price changes, defined as the first difference in the logs of prices. He found the distribution to be approximately normal

He also discovered that the standard deviation of log differences for various price series increased with the square root of time.

This discovery has two important results:

1. It provides evidence that log changes in prices are random.
2. It furnishes a rule for estimating the standard deviation, which is to say the variability or risk, of changes in prices.

33

It means, for example, that you can estimate the probability of losing half your money, or doubling it, in a year or five years.

The following tables illustrate what Osborne found.

Table 5.1 records the standard deviation of daily changes in the logs of the S&P 500 Index between 1980 and late 1986. We show the standard deviation for changes in price over ten intervals: 1, 2, 4, 8, 16, 32, 64 and 128 days.

Table 5.1 Standard & Poor 500 Index 1980–1986
Changes in the Logs of Daily Prices (×100)

(1) Time Interval in Days	(2) Square Root of Time Interval	(3) Standard Deviation of 1 day (×100)	(4) Estimated Standard Deviation (×100)	(5) Actual Standard Deviation (×100)
1	1	x .9 =	.9	.9
2	1.4	x .9 =	1.3	1.3
4	2	x .9 =	1.8	1.9
8	2.8	x .9 =	2.5	2.
16	4	x .9 =	3.6	3.8
32	5.7	x .9 =	5.1	5.3
64	8	x .9 =	7.2	7.5
128	11.3	x .9 =	10.2	11.0

The formula for estimating the standard deviation is given in columns 2, 3 and 4. The expected standard deviation is obtained by multiplying the standard deviation for 1 day by the square root of the number of days. The standard deviation for one day is .9. To obtain the value for 4 days, we multiply the .9 by the square root of 4, or by 2, and obtain 1.8. The estimated value 1.8 is shown in column 4. It compares with the actual value of 1.9 given in column 5.

The actual figures are the standard deviation of the changes in logs. We've arbitrarily multiplied the values by 100, which makes them comparable to the standard deviation of the percentage change in price. For changes under 15 percent, 100 × the log change is not far from the percent change.

A comparison of columns 4 and 5 reveals a close correspondence: the standard deviation rises with the square root of time, as we would expect if changes in stock prices behaved like a random variable.

The next test is for the standard deviation of changes in the logs of the closing price of General Motors common stock from 1976 to 1986. The results are given in Table 5.2.

Table 5.2 General Motors Common Stock 1976–1986
Changes in the Logs of Daily Prices (×100)

(1) Time Interval in Days	(2) Square Root of Time Interval	(3) Standard Deviation of 1 day (×100)	(4) Estimated Standard Deviation (×100)	(5) Actual Standard Deviation (×100)
1	1	× 1.45 =	1.4	1.4
2	1.4	× 1.45 =	2.0	2.1
4	2	× 1.45 =	2.9	3.0
8	2.8	× 1.45 =	4.1	4.0
16	4	× 1.45 =	5.8	5.5
32	5.7	× 1.45 =	8.2	7.7
64	8	× 1.45 =	11.6	11.0
128	11.3	× 1.45 =	16.4	15.0

There is clearly a close correspondence between the estimated standard deviation and the actual. The correspondence, given in the columns 4 and 5, lies in the simultaneous rise of the estimated and actual standard deviations with the square root of time.

What is the significance of this relationship for the investor? There are several important implications:

1. You can predict risk. That is, you can estimate the standard deviation for any period if you know it for one period. If you know it for weekly periods, you can estimate for monthly periods; if you know it for annual periods, you can estimate it for five- or ten-year periods—but not completely, and only with some caution. Statisticians will warn you about extrapolating beyond the period for which you have data. To calculate a standard deviation for a month, you need nearly a year of data. For a decade, you need eight to ten decades of data. Nevertheless, the square root rule seems to hold for a lot of periods and a lot of series.

2. Risk rises with time, but not as rapidly as time. Total risk rises with the square root of time.

3. However, the risk of your *average annual return* declines with time. The standard deviation of the total return rises with time, but the standard deviation of the *mean* declines with time.

The square root rule is important. It provides evidence of the random character of changes in stock prices. When we define risk as the standard deviation, the rule enables us to predict risk for different periods of time. It shows us how the risk of the stock market as a whole and of individual stocks changes with time.

The probable gains and losses of investing in stocks, described in tables later, will depend on the standard deviation. So the ability to predict the standard deviation for different time, or holding, intervals is crucial to assessing probable gains and losses.

CHAPTER 6

The Basic Model for the Stock Market

Changes in the price of a stock are influenced by two components, the market component and the stock component. If we know the distribution of these two components, then we can make some predictions about the the range of values of a market, or any stock, or any portfolio.

The distribution of the two components was approximately log normal and that (generally speaking) each component, the market and the stock, have equal weight. The resulting price series follows (again approximately) a random walk. That means that past changes in price provide no information about future changes in price.

Four statistical facts been shown:

1. The cross-sectional standard of changes in (the logs of) price will increase with the square root of time.

2. The standard deviation of the market changes in (the logs) of price will increase with the square root of time.

3. The mean change in the market will rise at a rate equal to the exponent of half the squared standard deviation—about 5 percent per year.

4. The standard deviation of the portfolio will decline to the standard deviation of the market component as the number of stocks in the portfolio increases.

Most of the literature on portfolio theory either assumes, or ignores, the first two facts above. The third fact, although it is the main statistical determinant of the mean rise in the market, has been largely ignored. Only the last point has been addressed, and that in unexpected ways and, on occasion, inaccurately.

The first two points enable you to determine the risk in any portfolio over any interval of time if you know the risk in a single interval. The third point lets you estimate the mean rise in the market. The fourth point lets you calculate the risk in a portfolio if you know the number of stocks it holds.

The following model fairly describes the stock market.

39

The Model

Changes in the price of a stock may be represented as the (antilogs of the) sum of two independent random elements, one peculiar to the stock, the other to the market. The expected value of these elements is zero and the standard deviation is about the same for each—roughly 18 percent per year.

These three equations describe what happens to the price of a stock or portfolio.

$$\text{standard deviation}^2 \quad s^2 \, \Delta \ln p = s_s^2 + s_m^2 \tag{1}$$

$$\text{mean change} = \exp{(s^2)/2} \tag{2}$$

$$\text{standard deviation} = \exp(4s^2/2)$$

$$\text{effect of time (holding period)} \quad s(t) = s(1)t^5 \tag{3}$$

where:

s is the standard deviation of (changes in the logs of price of) the portfolio;

s_s is the standard deviation peculiar to the stock;

s_m is the standard deviation peculiar to the market;

s(1) is the standard deviation in unit time; and

t is the holding period, or the time you hold the portfolio.

The expected mean of the log differences is zero, and the distribution of changes in the logs is approximately normal.

The model has several surprising features, which shall next be discussed.

The Mean Change

The expected change in the logs of price is zero, yet the expected change in price is positive. This apparent contradiction arises from the fact that when the underlying distribution of the logs is normal with an expected mean of zero, then the mean of the antilogs is positive and can be calculated from formula (2) above. Later we will simulate the results of an actual study of performance on all stocks in the New York Stock Exchange from 1926 to 1965 and show how they could be generated by formula (2).

Risk

Because the part of the change in price due to the stock and the part of the change in price due to the market are independent of each other, we can reduce, but not entirely eliminate the risk in a portfolio of stocks. Because components for different stocks are independent, we can reduce the risk of the portfolio mean by increasing the number of stocks in the portfolio. In doing this, we place equal investments in each stock. Because these influences—the stock influence and the market influence—are about the same, we can cut the risk, the standard deviation, *by about half* using a portfolio of a large number of equally weighted stocks. The actual formula for calculating the reduction in the standard deviation is:

$$s^2 = (s_m{}^2) + (s_s{}^2/n) \tag{4}$$

The first term in parentheses is the market risk, and it never declines. The second term changes when you add stocks. When the number of stocks (n) in the portfolio becomes very large, the second term approaches zero and the standard deviations of the total portfolio approaches the standard deviation of the market s(m).

Modern portfolio theory calls the market risk s(m) systematic risk because it affects all stocks the same way, i.e. systematically. Market risk, or systematic risk, cannot be reduced by adding additional common stocks. The residual risk attributed to individual stocks can be eliminated entirely by adding enough stocks.

With a large number of stocks, the portfolio risk becomes the following:

$$s = s(m) \tag{4a}$$

The final point to be made is that the standard deviation of returns rises with the square root of time. Quadruple the holding period and the standard deviation doubles. This fact is revealed by formula (3) above.

To sum up our discussion of risk, the model says that the standard deviation, s, of a portfolio:

1. declines when you add more stocks to the portfolio;
2. cannot decline to less than the market standard deviation s(m); and
3. increases with the square root of time, or the holding period t.

Implications of the Model

We will now examine what this model means for the effect of the number of securities on the risk of a portfolio. We will call the beginning risk 100 for a 1-year standard devaiation and we will change only n, the number of stocks. (See Table 6.1.)

**Table 6.1 Implication of the Model for the Effect of Increasing
            Number of Stocks In a Portfolio on the Standard Deviation
            of Return**

Number of Stocks	1	2	8	16	32	128	inf
Standard Deviation	100	85	68	63	59	54	50

Now we'll examine what the formula means for the effect of time on the risk of a portfolio. We will hold the number of stocks constant and increase the time interval or holding period. (See Table 6.2.)

**Table 6.2 Implication of the Model for the Effect of the Holding Period
            on the Standard Deviation of Return**

Time	1	2	3	4	5	10	20
Standard Deviation	100	141	173	200	224	316	447

As you go from 1 day to 4 days, or from 1 year to 4 years, the risk, as measured by the standard deviation of return, doubles in two ways. The market risk doubles and the risk across stocks doubles. In other words, not only does the standard deviation of the market rise, but the standard deviation across stocks rises. For a portfolio represented by Table 6.2 (100 = a stock portfolio of an infinite number of stocks), for a single stock all the numbers must be doubled, which would increase the standard deviation from 200 for 1 year to 400 for 4 years and 632 for 10 years.

The third statistical fact mentioned earlier (page 40) covers the mean. When the distribution of changes is log normal and expected mean of zero, the mean of the prices themselves is positive (with the exponent of one-half the standard deviation squared). This seems contradictory, but it is not. Although the mean expected change in the logs is zero, the mean expected change in the actual market is positive and entirely dependent the standard deviation. This is an important point.

The expected change in the logs of price is zero, but the expected change in the prices themselves is greater than zero. This apparent contradiction arises because the distribution of changes in stock prices is log normal; that is, the distribution of changes in the logs of prices is normal. When this is the case, the mean change in the log of price is zero, as noted above, but the mean change in the prices is positive.

A rough illustration of this is given by the probability of a price going from 100 to 200 and from 100 to 50. For stock prices, the probabilities of each are approximately the same. In the first case, the price doubles. In the second, it halves. The log change from 100 to 200 is +.69. The log change from 100 to 50 is −.69. Consequently the expected change in logs is the sum of these two values (+.69 and −.69), or zero. But the expected change in the antilogs is not zero, as shown below:

Initial Price	Final Price	Change	Log Change
100	200	+100	+.69
100	50	−50	−69
Mean change		+25	0

The mean change in price is +25, but the mean change in the logs of price is 0. That illustrates what happens with a log normal distribution.

We will now examine what the model implies using a (log) standard deviation of .35 for a single stock. That's about the same as a standard deviation of 18 percent per year for the market. (See Table 6.3.)

Table 6.3 Implication of the Model for the Expected Value of a Stock Portfolio at the End of Various Number of Years (t), where the Standard Deviation of the Stock is .35.

Holding Period Years	1	5	10	20	30	40	50
Expected Value	1.1	1.4	1.8	3.4	6.3	11.6	21.4

Table 6.3 means that if you started with $1 you would expect to have $3.40 at the end of 20 years and $21.40 at the end of 50 years—an increase arising solely from the fact that the standard deviation of changes in the logs was 0.35, the mean change in logs being zero. The conversion to antilogs causes the rise. While the increase in wealth may seem high, the return is only 6.3 percent per annum compound, by no means extraordinary. Moreover, there is still a 50/50 chance that you will have less than $1 at the end of 50 years. And the expected *median* value—as opposed to the expected *mean*—is still $1.

CHAPTER 7

Predicting the Distribution of Historical Returns on the Stock Market

The measure of market risk— the standard deviation of changes in the log of price—rises with the square root of time. This rule appears to hold for many different time series. It also appears to be invariant—it holds over any segment of the past. The square root rule is very useful. If you know the standard deviation for one period, you should be able to estimate it for any other period. If you know the standard deviation for daily changes in the Dow Jones Average, you should be able to calculate the standard deviation for weekly changes, or monthly changes, or yearly changes, and so on. If you know it for a month, you should be able to estimate it for a year, or five years.

It has also been shown that the distribution of changes in (the logs) of price is approximately normal. That being the case, we can estimate the probable proportion of changes in the market, up or down, of any degree. We should be able to estimate the distribution of changes in a market index, such as the Standard & Poor's 500.

Finally, it has been shown that any large sample of stocks with the same investment in each approximates the market to a high degree. Therefore, we should be able to use one market index to approximate another.

In fact, if the measure is truly invariant, we should be able to take changes in one series, say the Dow Jones Industrial Average over the past four years, and simulate the distribution of changes in another series, say Standard & Poor 500 over the last century.

That is exactly what we do in the following test. We take four years of daily data from the Dow Jones Industrial Average and estimate the distribution of annual returns of the Standard & Poor Index since 1880—nearly a century ago.

If the underlying nature of the data has not changed over the course of a century—if data is stationary, as the statisticians put it—then it doesn't matter whether you get your model in recent years and backtest it on earlier years, or vice-versa.

The test procedure **was** as follows:

1. Determine the standard deviation of daily changes in the logs of stock prices.

2. Assume that the distribution of changes are (log) normal with a standard deviation that increases with the square root of time.

3. Test these assumptions against another set of daily changes.

4. Test these assumptions against less frequent, but long-term data (monthly, for instance).

Imagine, for a moment, that long-term changes mirror short-term changes for this data. Suppose the distribution of changes is the same, and that the degree of change is larger—not different, only larger. Suppose there is only a change of scale. Suppose in all other respects things are the same. If we know what happens to daily changes, and we know the rule for converting from daily changes to monthly changes or yearly changes, we can predict the distribution of longer term changes. We can also predict the probability of a change of any magnitude.

This approach is the precise reverse of Mandelbrot's analysis of fractiles. Mandelbrot said that no matter how small a section of the data you take, that section resembles the larger section in all respects. In terms of what was suggested in the last paragraph, reducing the difference interval, in Mandelbrot's view, has no effect on the results. Here we argue the reverse. No matter how large the differencing interval, the distribution will be the same for a small interval except in terms of scale.

We sampled daily changes in the Dow for the standard deviation and then assumed two things: 1) that the distribution of daily changes (in the ln) of price is normal; and 2) that the standard deviation rises with the square root of time. We then tested the normal distribution derived from the sample of daily changes in the Dow first against two samples of the same series for different periods and then against annual changes in the Standard & Poor monthly index, 1883–1985. As our sample for deriving the standard deviation, we used the Dow for the years 1980–82. We tested the results of that sample against the Dow for 1983–85. Here we predicted forward using daily changes to predict subsequent daily changes.

Then we tested backward using daily changes not to predict subsequent daily changes but rather to estimate prior *annual* changes in an *entirely different* market average. We used the Dow Jones daily data for making the estimate. Using this daily data and the square root rule, we estimated the distribution of annual changes for approximately one-hundred years 1883–

Plot using Excel

1985. Thus we tested backward. You will note some overlap in the Dow and the S&P data, three years, representing roughly 3 percent of the S&P data.

Tables 7.1 and 7.2 show proportions predicted by the method, along with the actual proportions.

Table 7.1 Estimation of Daily Changes in Dow Jones Average 1983–86 Based on Daily Changes 1979–82

Percent Change Over	Estimated Proportion	Actual Proportion
–1.5	95	97
–1.2	90	94
–0.6	75	80
0	50	49
0.6	25	19
1.2	10	8
1.7	5	4

Table 7.2 Estimation of Annual Changes in S&P 500 1883–1985 Based on Daily Changes in Dow Jones Average 1983–86

Percent Change Over	Estimated Proportion	Actual Proportion
–20	95	88
–16	90	82
– 9	75	70
0	50	53
9	25	33
18	10	18
24	5	10

Careful study of this data reveals that there is a close correspondence between predicted and actual frequencies. It is remarkable that we are able to predict annual frequencies on one series from daily data on another series; that we were able to predict frequencies over the course of a century from data over the course of four years; that we were able to predict changes over 250 trading days from data over the course of a single trading day. This ability to predict from such disparate samples suggests that there are some inherent characteristics of the stock market that can be induced from the general characteristics of probability. We can predict the probabilities.

The importance of this demonstration is that it shows we can use a short sequence of data to predict a long sequence. Even though we do not have enough data to determine, say, the distribution of 10-year changes in the market, we will probably not be too far off if we take estimates of the distribution of monthly changes and then, using the square root rule and the normal distribution, make an approximate estimate of the 10-year distribution. In other words, we use short-term changes in the market to estimate the distribution of long-term changes. What we have shown suggests that the market is, in Mandelbrot's words, statistically self-similar to a remarkable degree.

CHAPTER 8

How to Reduce Common Stock Portfolio Risk

The risk in a portfolio of common stocks may be reduced by increasing the number of stocks in the portfolio and placing an equal investment in each stock. Doing this can reduce the risk of the portfolio by one-half—at least statistically. Further reduction in risk is not possible if the portfolio is restricted to common stocks. The reduction in risk assumes that the stocks in the portfolio have no common influences, apart from that of the market itself. If there are common influences, such as might arise if the stocks are in the same industry, then the degree of reduction in risk will be diminished. Attention to industry diversification can sharply curtail industry risk.

The mathematics of risk reduction were first presented formally by Markowitz, though the idea is common to basic statistical theory. If we take out the market effect on changes in common stock prices, we are left with a residual price change. That residual price change may be considered a random variable. The standard deviation is a good measure of risk. By definition, the standard deviation of the average of a sum of random variables is that average divided by the square root of the number of components. The equation of the relationship is the following:

standard deviation = $average/n^5$

Using this formula, we can actually state the reduction in the standard deviation achieved by increasing the number of stocks.

The theoretical reduction in the residual risk of the portfolio is shown in the right-hand column, which is $1/n^5$. There are several interesting features of the effect of adding stocks to the portfolio:

1. The second stock provides the greatest reduction in risk.

2. Each additional stock provides less reduction in risk than its predecessor.

3. By the time we add the ninth stock, we have reduced residual risk to one-third the original risk.

4. To cut risk to one-tenth the original, 100 stocks are needed in the portfolio.

Table 8.1 Reduction in Residual Risk as the Number of Stocks Rises

Number of Stocks n	Reduction in Residual Risk $1/n^{.5}$
1	1.00
2	.70
3	.57
4	.50
5	.45
10	.31
15	.26
20	.22
30	.18
50	.14
100	.10
1000	.03

The practical impact of the theoretical effect is that additional stocks can have a dramatic effect on portfolio risk reduction. We can compare the theoretical reduction in risk to actual reduction by looking at the effect of portfolios created by randomly picking various numbers of stocks and placing an equal investment in each. The measure of risk is the standard deviation. Since the return is a single period return, the market has no effect and we have a perfect test of Table 8.1.

For that comparison, we will use the data from the Lorie Fisher study of all New York Stock Exchange Stocks 1945–65. The results for two 10-year holding periods are shown in Table 8.2.

There is a quite remarkable correspondence between the expected and actual reduction in risk. The results for the period 1926–45 are not at all as close; I suspect the reason is that the much smaller sample available for the earlier period curtailed the reduction in risk.

Table 8.2 neglects the effect of the market on risk. Market risk, fluctuations in the Dow Jones Average or the Standard & Poor 500, account for about half the risk in a portfolio. It is not possible to eliminate this risk. We can make a simple study of risk by examining what happens to the standard deviation of a portfolio when both the number of stocks and market risk are considered simultaneously. Table 8.3 simulates this effect.

Table 8.2 Expected and Actual Reduction in Standard Deviation with Increase in Number of Stocks

Number of Stocks	Standard Deviation Reported of Wealth Ratios	Expected Reduction in Standard Deviation	Actual Reduction in Standard Deviation
1	2.571	100	100
2	1.820	71	71
8	.917	35	36
16	.653	25	25
32	.469	18	18
128	.256	9	10

Table 8.3 Market, Stock, and Total Standard Deviation for Portfolios of Various Numbers of Stocks

Number of Stocks	Market Standard Deviation	Individual Stock Standard Deviation	Total Standard Deviation
1	50	50	100
2	50	35	85
3	50	29	79
4	50	25	75
5	50	22	72
6	50	20	70
7	50	19	69
8	50	18	68
9	50	17	67
10	50	16	66
16	50	13	63
32	50	9	59
128	50	4	54
inf	50	0	50

In this table, the total standard deviation is assumed to be equal to the sum of the market standard deviation and the stock standard deviation. Strictly speaking, the total variance (s^2) should be equal to the sum of the variances, but the formula used in the table appears to work as well.

Based on the standard deviation reported in the Fisher Lorie study, reduction for 1-year returns for the total sample over the 1926–65 period are shown in Table 8.4.

Table 8.4 Effect of Increasing the Number of Stocks on the Standard Deviation of Portfolios (Fisher Lorie Study)

Number of Stocks	Standard Deviation of Wealth Ratios	Expected Reduction in Standard Deviation	Actual Reduction in Standard Deviation
1	.554	100	100
2	.451	85	81
8	.354	68	64
16	.335	63	60
32	.325	59	58
128	.318	54	57

Clearly, there is a fairly good correspondence between the expected reduction in the standard deviation achieved by increasing the number of stocks and the actual reduction.

A later study by Evans and Archer, covering S&P 500 stocks between January 1958 and July 1959, reveals similar results. Their findings, together with the expected results, are shown in Table 8.5.

Evans and Archer restricted their sample portfolios to a maximum of 40 stocks. Though they did not give the actual results, they did give the formula from which we have calculated the standard deviation. As has been shown, the expected and actual reductions in the standard deviations are fairly close to one another.

Summary

When you invest in stocks, you can cut your risk by diversifying—by adding more stocks to your portfolio and placing an equal investment in each stock. The major reductions in risk come from adding the first few stocks. After 10 or 15 stocks, the degree of reduction achieved by adding more stocks declines. The main objective is to add stocks and achieve thereby some diversification—and cut your risk.

Table 8.5 Effect of Increasing the Number of Stocks on the Standard Deviation of Portfolios (Evans Archer Study)

Number of Stocks	Standard Deviation Annualized from Formula	Expected Reduction in Standard Deviation	Actual Reduction in Standard Deviation
1	.290	100	100
2	.220	85	79
8	.184	68	63
16	.177	63	61
32	.172	59	59
40	.171	58	59

CHAPTER 9

Are There Changes in Stock Market Volatility?

Our ability to predict stock market risk assumes that risk doesn't change from one historical period to the next. If the volatility of the market is comparatively stable (say within a factor of two) then we can use past measures of the standard deviation to predict future measures. If this is not the case, then we cannot make a very good prediction about future volatility. Consequently, the question of stability of the variability of the market is critical to prediction.

Certainly one has to take account of the level of the market when measuring volatility, or when estimating the standard deviation. In recent markets where the Dow Jones Industrial Average exceeded 2,500, daily changes of 30, even 50, were not unusual. When the market was 600, a daily change of that magnitude would have been extraordinary. Dollar changes in the market depend on the level of the market because the distribution of changes is log normal—which means that percentage changes, or log changes, will not be affected by the level of the market; only absolute dollar amounts. Measuring the standard deviation using percentages, or equivalent rates of return, will provide a measure which is not arbitrarily affected by the level of the market.

Even a cursory glance at a chart of the stock market over a long period suggests that the volatility of the market does change. For our purpose, the real question is the magnitude of the changes.

The first person to study changes in volatility was R.R. Officer. Officer examined the standard deviation of monthly returns of the Dow Jones Industrial Average from 1897 to 1969. During this period, the standard deviation was generally above 5 percent and rarely exceeded 16 percent, except during the stock market crash of 1929, when it reached twice that figure. Thus, there was a fair degree of stability to the risk in the market, with the notable exception of the period surrounding October 1929.

61

Table 9.1 shows the standard deviation of monthly changes in the Standard & Poor's 500 Stock Price Index over the period 1883-1982. These tables show the standard deviation of changes in the logs of the market index. There is variation in the standard deviation, but it is limited; it ranges between 5.4 and 16.4, or within a factor of 3. Most of the time the range is between 6 and 10, a much smaller range than suggested by the extreme values.

As the table reveals, the market volatility is certainly not invariant: the standard deviation does change from one period to the next. But there seem to be bounds to the shifts in variability. The standard deviation appears to remain within a factor of roughly 2. Our measures of volatility appear to be sufficiently constant to allow us to estimate future standard deviations, recognizing, of course, that there will be occasional periods when volatility will be much higher than the past average suggests. Overall, the standard deviation is sufficiently within bounds to permit reasonable estimation of future volatility.

Table 9.1 Standard Deviation of Changes In Log of Standard & Poor's 500 Common Stock Index 1883–1982 (×100)

Years	Standard Deviation (×100)
1883–1892	5.7
1893–1902	6.5
1903–1912	8.1
1913–1922	7.0
1923–1932	16.4
1933–1942	10.4
1943–1952	7.2
1953–1962	8.2
1963–1972	5.4
1973–1982	8.6

CHAPTER 10

Predicting Probable Returns
from a Single Stock

Suppose you want to know what you can expect to gain if you invest in a certain stock. You can't get an exact return, but (surprisingly to some), you can determine the various probable returns.

It isn't difficult. To make a probability estimate of returns from buying a single stock, you must know three things. First, you must know the standard deviation of past changes in the price of the stock. Then you must know the time interval over which the probability estimate is to be made. Finally, you need the mean expected change which we will assume to be zero. With this data, and the Probability Tables, you can find the probability of any degree of change.

The steps are as follows:

1. Secure prices for a series of equally spaced intervals.

2. Compute percentage changes in the price of the stock over a those intervals.

3. Calculate the standard deviation of the percentage price changes.

4. Multiply the standard deviation by one of the following numbers:

Weekly prices	7.2
Monthly prices	3.5
Annual prices	1.0

5. Look up the probability of changes in the Probability Tables (Appendix II).

Table 10.1 provides an example —first obtain percent changes and calculate the standard deviation. The standard deviation of the percent change in price in the example is 38 percent. We needn't multiply the standard deviation by the appropriate factor, since we have annual changes.

Next, we turn to the Probability Tables (in Appendix II). Rounding off 38 percent, we will use the column labeled 40 percent. The data in Table 10.2 is taken from Appendix Table IIa for 1-year periods for a 40-percent standard deviation.

**Table 10.1 Example of Finding the Standard Deviation of the Change
                    In the Price of a Stock**

Dec 31	Price	Percent Change
1981	42	
1982	49	17%
1983	63	29
1984	50	−21
1985	27	−46
1986	44	63
1987	52	18
Standard Deviation	38.4%	

Table 10.2 Standard Deviation of 40% One Year In the Future

Rise of at Least	Probability (%) of Rise
200%	—
150	0%
100	3
90	3
80	4
70	6
60	8
50	11
40	16
30	22
20	29
10	39
0	50

Fall of at Least	Probability of Fall
0	50%
-10	36
-20	25
-30	14
-40	6
-50	2
-60	0

In Table 10.2, the left column shows the rise (or fall). The right column shows the probability of a rise (or fall) of at least that shown. For a rise of at least 60 percent, the probability is 8 percent. The probably is 6 percent of a fall of at least 40 percent.

The table provides an idea of what the odds are, based on a 1-year period. If you want a longer period, say two or five years, use the data in the table for those periods. The standard deviations in the table are all based on a 1-year standard deviation.

The table is based on the assumption that the distribution of changes in the price of a stock conforms to a log normal distribution. Though technically we should compute the standard deviation of changes in the logs of price, we get a reasonably good answer simply using percentage changes since for changes under 15 percent—which most changes are—the log change is approximately the same.

Sometimes you can obtain the standard deviation directly from another source, without calculating it yourself. In that case, provided you have an annual standard deviation, you can refer directly to the Probability Table.

◆ ◆ ◆

An estimate of probable returns from buying one stock will tell you several things. It will tell you the probability of any particular gain, like doubling your money in one year, or in ten; or increasing your investment by 10 percent in the next six months, or two years. It will also tell you the probability of losing money on the investment—losing half your investment, for example, in the next year, or in the next decade; or losing 10 percent in the next half-year. It will tell you whether the odds of a positive return are better than the flip of a coin, or not. The estimate gives you the probability of various things happening once you order your broker to purchase the stock and send your check to your broker.

The probability estimate *won't* tell you some things you might like to know. It won't tell you how much you will gain. The probability estimate will enable you to check assertions on odds made by someone else. If someone tells you that there is a 90 percent chance of doubling your money, the table will tell you the odds of that happening. The table won't tell you what *will* happen. It gives you the *probability* of something happening. Not a definite answer—only the probability.

CHAPTER 11

Estimating Probable Returns on a Mutual Fund

How can we calculate the probable returns from investing in a mutual fund?

Most mutual funds are appraised on the basis of their past performance record, generally over the last year, three years, five years, or decade. The mutual fund rating services generally give these statistics and will rank mutual funds on the basis of the overall record over an interval of time. Mutual fund advertisements, which are restricted in the kind and method of presentation, provide this kind of record. But the total return over a period is not the best way to guage the future, however appealing it may seem.

Not only that, but most funds' records vary widely from one year to the next, or for one decade to the next. Very few mutual funds, for example, win top honors every year for a decade. Not many mutual funds remain in the top quartile, even the top half, for ten years running.

The best fund is often the most volatile—the one with a good probability of really crashing when the market drops. A fund at the top of the list in an up market is often a roller coaster fund that will bounce around like a yo-yo.

Mutual funds will behave just like the market, but will often be more volatile, unless it is an Index fund designed to mirror the S&P 500 or another index.

To see how volatile a fund is, you can look at the standard deviation of annual returns, preferably for seven or eight years (if you can get that much data). You can also work up the standard deviation from monthly data, or weekly data, or even daily data.

The annual returns on a typical mutual fund are given on Table 11.1. The return includes both dividends received plus change in market value expressed as a percent of the fund value at the beginning of the year. Returns are expressed in percent.

The standard deviation of the above changes is 34 percent. The method of calculating the standard deviation is given in Appendix V.

Table 11.1 Example of Annual Returns on a Mutual Fund

Year	Annual Return
1986	+80
1985	+15
1984	+10
1983	− 25
1982	+ 5
1981	− 20
1980	+17

To get the probabilities, go to the Probability Table. Look up the column under the standard deviation of 35 percent for 1 year in the future. The 35 percent is close enough to the 34-percent actual. You can use Table 11.2.

Table 11.2 Standard Deviation 35% One Year In Future

Increase of at Least	Probability %
100%	1
90	2
80	3
70	4
60	6
50	9
40	13
30	19
20	27
10	38
0	50

Decrease of at Least	Probability %
0	50
−10	36
−20	23
−30	12
−40	4
−50	1

The table gives you the probabilities of gain or loss for a mutual fund with a standard deviation of 35 percent. There is a 50-percent probability it will rise—and an equal probability that it will fall. There is a 1-percent probability that it will rise by 100 percent—double—and an equal, or a 1-percent probability, that it will halve—fall by 50 percent. That gives you some idea of the risk. The chance of a 30-percent fall is 12 percent, or 1 in 8. The tables are based on the assumption that the returns have a log-normal distribution.

The table gives probable returns for one year in the future.

What about longer periods? For longer periods you have to use one of the other tables. There are tables for 1, 2, 3, 4, 5, 10, and 15 years. For longer periods, you can also multiply the standard deviation by the square root of the number of years for a new standard deviation. Find the appropriate column for the new standard deviation, then look up the probabilities as before to determine what your potential risks rewards are likely to be.

Note that in the table the positive and negative probabilities are not the same. Only the log changes are equal.

CHAPTER 12

Predicting the Probability of Loss

Estimating the probability of loss is similar to finding the probable changes in the price of a stock, or probable future returns on a fund, or probable changes in profit margins. But there is a slight twist to the matter that alters the computation.

In finding the probability of loss we look at the probability distribution of future changes in profits in relation to how far they are now above, or below, zero profits. We measure the distance above, or below, zero profits by the standard deviation—the standard deviation of changes in profits. And we use the normal distribution to find the probability of a change in profits large enough to reduce profits to zero or below, or keep profits below zero.

Loss, in the sense used here, means negative profits, the failure of a company to earn a profit. By profit we mean reported earnings after deducting amortization and depreciation, or more specifically, the earnings from which dividends are paid. We also mean profits exclusive of non-current items, such as extraordinary write-offs. This definition is not sacred to the method described here, for the same method may be applied to other definitions of profit and loss, or to cash flow, or to the probability of negative cash flow, or to negative earnings before interest charges, or to whatever interests you. Whatever your definition, the methodology is the same.

To find the probability of loss, take the following steps.

1. Collect 7 or more years of earnings data.
2. Compute annual changes in earnings. ($a \nu \cdot t \! \! h \ d e b t$)
3. Find the standard deviation of the changes in earnings.
4. Divide the most recent annual earnings figure by the standard deviation to obtain what in statistics is called the z-score.
5. From the table of *Probability of Loss* (Table 12.3), find the probability of loss.

If profits are positive, use the part of the table for positive profit. If profits are negative, use the part of the table for negative profits.

This procedure gives you the probability of a loss in the forthcoming year.

77

Let's take an example:

1. Collect 7 or more years of earnings data.

2. Compute annual changes in earnings (as in Table 12.1).

Table 12.1 Example of Earnings Per Share and Change In Earnings Per Share of a Company

Year	Earnings	Change in Earnings
1981	1.21	—
1982	1.80	+ 0.59
1983	0.75	− 1.05
1984	0.05	− 0.70
1985	0.57	+ 0.52
1986	0.40	− 0.17
1987	0.15	− 0.25

3. Find the standard deviation of changes.

Standard Deviation = 0.65

4. Determine how many standard deviations above, or below, zero earnings the most recent earnings figure is by dividing the latest profit figure by the standard deviation.

We divide the latest earnings figure, $0.15, by the standard deviation, $0.65, giving 0.23. This is the z-score, defined as a quantity divided by its standard deviation:

z-score = 0.15/0.65

$\quad\quad\quad$ = 0.23

5. From table of the Probability of Loss (Table 12.3), find the probability for a company whose earnings are positive. The table shows that for a z-score of 0.25 the probability of loss is 40% (see Table 12.2). For a z-score of .20 the probability is 42%. So the probability of loss is between these two figures, or about 41%:

Probability of loss = 41%

6. If profits are negative, use the portion of the table for negative profits. In making the computation, we used reported earnings per share. The same kind of computation could have been applied using another measure of profits, such as actual profits in millions of dollars, profit margins, return on total assets, or even percentage changes in profits.

Table 12.2 Probability of Loss Positive Earnings

Earnings/Standard Deviation of Earnings z-score	Probability of Loss %
.00	50%
.05	48
.10	46
.15	44
.20	42
.25	40
.30	38
.35	36
.40	34
.50	31
.60	27
.70	24
.80	21
.90	18

It's normally best to use reported profits as they are reported in per share figures or total dollars, as we did above. But if there are large shifts in profits, as might occur from a merger, then make an adjustment. You can do this by dividing profits by assets to get return on assets, or by sales to get profit margins. Then use the new series just as we used the earnings per share figures above: find the change in margins each year; compute the standard deviation of changes in margins; and finally divide the latest margin by the standard deviation to obtain the z-score. Then look up the z-score in the table.

Using profit margins, or return on total assets, or return on equity, gives you a figure that is not affected by an enormous and arbitrary changes in the corporation as a result of mergers or acquisitions. In a long study of the probability of loss, we used earnings/assets in order to obtain comparable figures for a large group of companies. This transformation may not be necessary, though it did homogenize the data.

What is needed in assessing the probability of loss is a measure of the variability of earnings and then a measure of how far profits are, by the latest figure, above or below zero. The latest figure is generally the best measure of future profits. By standardizing that figure as a z-score by dividing it by the standard deviation of changes, you can apply the normal curve to estimate the probability of loss. You can also make forecasts of the probability of loss in future years by multiplying the standard deviation by the square root of the number of years after completing step 2. Then proceed as before, and you have your answer.

The probability of loss that you derive by the above method has a number of significant advantages over other measures. The probability for one company is strictly comparable with the probability of another, irrespective of what industry the companies happen to be drawn from. The measure is not affected by arbitrary scaling of the variables as are other measures of credit risk, like the Altman's z-score. Loss, the absence of profits, is a good indicator of problems, like nonpayment of interest or principal on a loan, future cuts in the dividend, and even bankruptcy.

So if the performance of a particular company concerns you, the first thing you should do is compute the probability of loss using the method described above.

Table 12.3 Tables for Finding Probability of Loss Probability of Loss

Positive Earnings

Earnings/Standard Deviation of Changes in Earnings z-score	Probability of Loss %
.00	50%
.05	48
.10	46
.15	44
.20	42
.25	40
.30	38
.35	36
.40	34
.50	31
.60	27
.70	24
.80	21
.90	18
1.00	16
1.10	14
1.20	11
1.30	10
1.40	8
1.50	7
1.60	6

Positive Earnings (continued)

Earnings/Standard Deviation of Changes in Earnings z-score	Probability of Loss %
1.70	5
1.80	4
1.90	3
2.00	2
2.25	1

Negative Earnings

Earnings/Standard Deviation of Changes in Earnings z-score	Probability of Loss %
.00	50
.05	52
.10	54
.15	56
.20	58
.25	60
.30	62
.35	64
.40	66
.50	69
.60	73
.70	76
.80	79
.90	82
1.00	84
1.10	86
1.20	88
1.30	90
1.40	92
1.50	93
1.60	95
1.70	96
1.80	96
1.90	97
2.00	98
2.25	99

CHAPTER 13

Predicting Probable Changes in Earnings

A Scenario

I'll never forget that year. It was a year of little snow, a year in which ice boaters took vacations in January so they could spend their days racing across the clear frozen stretches of Lake Minnetonka. It was also a year when companies that made snow-plowing equipment reeled as if hit by the plague, for the dry winter ravaged revenues and sent earnings below zero.

Harry Sutch had come to see me the previous summer. Harry is the most unanalytical-looking securities analyst you'd ever hope to meet: short and heavyset, with thick eyebrows over sleepy looking eyes, always dressed in a rumpled tweed sports coat that never matched his slacks. The appearance was misleading, for Harry always penetrated to the bottom of things. He wouldn't stop until he had.

I was just an early stop on his route to investigating one company or another. He had slouched in the nearest leather chair and explained that the *Farmers Almanac* predicted a dry winter coming up. He wondered how it might affect the snow-blower companies. If they got hit by a snow drought, it would drive their earnings underground.

I knew the bad earnings wouldn't hit the papers for a year, because the drop would take place in the March quarter. That would be reported in June since it takes about three months before the figures are reported. If the *Farmers Almanac* proved right, the snow industry would have trouble. The question was, how much trouble? How far could earnings drop?

"That's why I came to you," Harry said. "I remembered you'd figured out how to estimate the volatility of earnings and their levels for various probabilities. I would want to know what the downside risk is."

I then explained how to make the estimate: Gather seven or eight years of earnings data. Then get your calculator and calculate the percent change from year to year so you've got six or seven changes in earnings per share.

Then I laid out the data (as shown in Table 13.1).

Table 13.1 Earnings Per Share and Percent Changes in Earnings

Year	Earnings per Share	Percent Change
1980	0.86	
1981	0.92	+ 7
1982	1.13	+ 23
1983	1.02	− 10
1984	1.25	+ 23
1985	0.97	− 22
1986	1.20	+ 24

The second column gives earnings per share. The third column gives the percent change in earnings per share.

Next, the standard deviation of the right-hand column—the annual percent changes in earnings—we computed. I worked it out with a calculator that could compute the standard deviation. The standard deviation turned out to be 20 percent.

Then we turned to a table showing the probability of various percentage changes for that standard deviation.

The relevant material from the table [Appendix II.a in this book] are in Table 13.2. The numbers in the right-hand column are probabilities.

Table 13.2 20% Standard Deviation 1 Year In Future

Fall of at Least	Probability (%)
0%	50
−5	39
−10	28
−20	11
−30	3
40	—

There is an 11 percent chance of at least a 20 percent fall in earnings and a 3 percent chance of at least a 30 percent drop in earnings.

Harry noted that if the 3 percent chance of a 30 percent fall occurred, there would be serious problems. And if the snow didn't stay next winter, the 3 percent would underestimate the odds.

His expression combined satisfaction and grimness.

"I know now what the odds are," he said at last. "That helps a lot. It gives me a solid estimate of the probabilities—which is just what I needed."

Prediction Changes in Earnings

Earnings are perhaps the most important variable affecting a corporation, whether in the form of stock price, the payment of dividends, the payment of interest and repayment of principal, or, in the end, the very continuance of the organization and its provision of goods and services and employment to its employees. For these reasons, earnings are very important.

In attempting to evaluate the corporation, it is important to make some kind of statement about future earnings. That, of course, means forecasting the range of probable changes in earnings.

The procedure described above is the same procedure we use in forecasting changes in other variables, like stock prices or the future probable returns on a mutual fund. It involves the following steps:

1. Obtain a series of earnings figures for the past seven or more years, if possible.

2. Compute annual changes in earnings. You can use percent changes provided that none of the earnings figures are zero or negative. You can also use changes in the logs, though that may not be necessary.

3. Calculate the standard deviation of the changes in earnings.

If some of the earnings figures are negative you can use the actual figures to calculate the standard deviation and then express the resulting standard deviation as a percent of the latest earnings figure.

4. Look up the probable changes in the Table of Probability given in Appendix II.

CHAPTER 14

Predicting Probable Changes
in Profit Margins

A Scenario: Predicting Probable Changes in Profit Margins

Some people are born optimists. They always look at the positive side of things, sure that whatever they do—or buy—will turn out well. Bob was one such person. He was forever optimistic, about life in general, but particularly about the industry in which he had spent his life's work—the television industry.

His rosy view of the future of the prices of television stations was typical. When television stations were selling at 10 times operating cash flow, Bob was sure the price would rise to 12 times operating cash flow. When station prices rose to 12 times, he was certain the next price would be 14 times operating cash flow.

"The prices," he liked to say, "reflect the inevitable growth of the television industry. Ad revenues rose with inflation, only at a faster rate. An annual 10 percent rise in operating margins was foreordained. The more likely figure will be 20 percent," he would say.

His firm belief in these matters was an article of faith. He had seen it happen for two decades. He saw no reason, therefore, for the growth not to continue.

Bob and I had a mutual friend who was a director of a television station. The friend came to me one day with a question that related to Bob's optimistic view of the industry.

"We're looking at acquiring a new television station in a regional city," he said. "Bob is very much for it. But I'm concerned that we can't afford to make the purchase."

"What's the problem?"

"The buyer wants a high price for the station. We don't know what the asking price is, but we think it's on the order of $18 million. We also figured we'd have to bid that high to beat three other bidders."

"Eighteen million," I repeated, "That is high."

"It is," he continued, "though how high it is depends on what the television station is earning."

"What is it earning?"

"The relevant figure is the price to operating cash flow. A price of $18 million is 20 times projected operating cash flow."

"That's much higher than the usual 12 or 14 times," I said.

"Exactly," he replied. "The only way we can make the deal work, particularly factoring in the interest costs on the debt we'd have to take on, is to raise margins."

"Raise them how much?"

"Substantially. From 27 percent to 35 percent."

"How can you do it?"

"Well, Bob says the industry average is 35 percent. This station's margins at 27 percent are well below the industry. Bob thinks that by cutting unnecessary costs, we should not have a difficult time bringing the station up to the industry average."

He paused for a moment, and then continued.

"That's why I wanted to see you. I want to know what you think the likelihood is of raising margins from 27 percent to 35 percent."

"The first thing to do is to look at past margins, see what they look like, and see how changeable they are."

The margins he showed me are given in Table 14.1.

Table 14.1 Profit Margins and Changes in Profit Margins

Year	Profit Margin	Change in Profit Margin
1980	25 %	
1981	27	+ 2 %
1982	19	− 8
1983	22	+ 3
1984	29	+ 7
1985	21	− 8
1986	27	+ 6

"Now," I said, "to get some kind of idea of the probability that margins can be raised from the latest figure of 27 percent to 35 percent, look at how much margins have changed in the past.

"Begin by putting annual changes in margins down [shown in the right-hand column]. Then look at the magnitude of past changes. If they are all much lower than the 8 percent change, then there isn't much chance of making that big a change. But if past changes are as much as 8 percent or more, then there might be a good chance.

"You can actually calculate the probability of reaching a margin of 35 percent from the data. You see how many standard deviations are involved in the change from 28 percent to 35 percent. Then you look up the probability of getting that many standard deviations from a table of the normal probability curve."

"Let's first find the standard deviation," I continued. I did the calculation on my calculator and came up with a figure of approximately 7 percent. "Here's what we do."

Then I went over the steps:

1. Find the amount of change required to go from 27 percent to 35 percent. We've done that already. It's 8 percent.

2. Compute the standard deviation of past changes. That's the standard deviation of those changes in the right column above.

Standard deviation of changes in margins = 7%

3. Divide the required change, the 8 percent, by the standard deviation of past changes, or by 7 percent.

Change in margins/standard deviation:

$$= 8/7$$
$$= 1.14$$
$$= z\text{-score}$$

"So, to hit the 35 percent margin, margins have to increase 1.14 standard deviation," he said.

"That's right," I replied.

"What then is the probability of moving 1.14 standard deviations?" my friend asked.

"You can look it up in a table of the normal curve." (See Table 14.2.)

The z-score of 1.14 lies between 1.10 and 1.20. The corresponding probabilities are 14 percent and 11 percent. The probability of raising margins by 8 percent was therefore 12 to 13 percent.

My friend looked a little worried.

Table 14.2 Table for Finding Probability of Change in Margins

Change in Margin/ Standard Deviation of Change z-score	Probability of Change %
.00	50
.05	48
.10	46
.15	44
.20	42
.25	40
.30	38
.35	36
.40	34
.50	31
.60	27
.70	24
.80	21
.90	18
1.00	16
1.10	14
1.20	11
1.30	10
1.40	8
1.50	7
1.60	6
1.70	5
1.80	4
1.90	3
2.00	2
2.25	1

(handwritten note beside table: 1.15 = 12.5% = 1/8)

"Though Bob will think that's easy," he said with a trace of concern in his voice, "I don't think it will be. After all, margins can go down as well as up. And they've never been at 35 percent before."

I nodded in agreement. He had an objective estimate of what the probability was of improving margins by that amount. The numbers were not that reassuring.

"It's possible," I agreed. "But not easy."

It's a good method to quantify a possibility. It can be used whenever one wants to know what the odds are of improving margins by a given amount.

CHAPTER 15

How to Estimate the Average Future Return from Stocks

What will the future return from stocks be? The fact is, we don't know precisely—and whatever estimate we make will most likely be wrong. Yet it is essential to make some kind of estimate of the long-run return of the stock market. What's the right way to do it and what's the wrong way? Unfortunately, the wrong way is very prevalent today.

There are two methods of estimating the long-run average return on stocks. One method is to calculate it from the standard deviation. The second is to estimate the mean from past returns. Each method has advantages and disadvantages.

The first method is the easiest. But it presumes we know the cross-sectional standard deviation of changes in the logs of stock prices. The distribution of changes in the logs of stock prices is a normal distribution. When we calculate returns on stock prices, we calculate them from the prices themselves, not from the logs. When you have a distribution whose logs are normal, the mean of the antilogs is given by the exponent of one-half the squared standard deviation, or:

mean = exp (average + standard deviation^2/2).

If we assume the average is zero, then the formula becomes:

mean = exp (standard deviation^2/2)

where the standard deviation is computed as the just difference in the logs of prices across stocks, or as the cross-sectional standard deviation.

Based on the second formula, mean changes in the market for various standard deviations—assuming the mean change in the log is zero—are as shown in Table 15.1.

When the standard deviation is 0.30, the expected mean change is 4.6 percent per year.

When the cross-sectional standard deviation of annual changes in the logs of prices is 0.35, the mean is 6.3 percent. If we estimate the cross-sectional standard deviation from the Fisher Lorie data (see Chapter 16) on all New York Stock Exchange common stocks from 1926 to 1972, we obtain 0.345 which results in a mean annual price rise of 6.1 percent.

The above assumes a mean change of zero in the logs of prices. If there is a mean change, use the first equation above. If you use the .30 figure above, which seems reasonable, you obtain a rounded figure of about 5 percent per year. Add the dividend, and your total return works out to be more like 8 percent. That's one good approach to finding the expected long-run return from the stock market.

Over the long-run, the returns on a return of 4.6 percent can be remarkable. One thousand dollars invested at the time of the Declaration of Independence was signed would be worth $13,288,599 today.

Table 15.1 Estimates of the Annual Mean Change in the Stock Market from Various Standard Deviations of the Mean Change in the Natural Logarithms

Standard Deviation	Mean Change
.10	0.5%
.15	1.1
.20	2.0
.25	3.2
.30	4.6
.35	6.3
.40	8.3
.45	10.7
.50	13.3

The second method of estimating the long-run rate of return is to look at actual changes in the market, with or without an adjustment for dividends. The important thing in using this method is to not count the same evidence twice. We discussed this briefly in Chapter 1. Don't double count; that is, don't calculate the mean change several times and use some of the same data more than once. It's not infrequent to see the same data used eight or ten times. It's done by using overlapping intervals. It is very common. But it is *very misleading*. If there is anything two centuries of effort in the statistical theory of measurement has discovered, it's that you must take independent samples. Otherwise, you have a biased sample and you can't measure the probable error of your result.

Let's look at the S&P 500 since the early 1900s and show what to do—and what not to do.

The first two columns were taken directly from an actual presentation of what the market would do. The same kind of presentation is used in the well-known Ibbotson-Sinquefield work. It is the wrong way to estimate because the data is not independent. The periods overlap excessively: the level of the market in 1986, for example, appears in every figure. That multiple use of the same ending date biases the results. Not only that, but you can't measure the probable error using this method.

**Table 15.2 How to Measure the Mean Change in the Stock Market
(average compound annual rates)**

Overlapping Periods	Mean Return	Independent Periods	Mean Return
1977–86	13.7	1977–86	13.7
1967–86	10.1	1967–76	6.6
1957–86	9.8	1957–66	9.2
1947–86	11.9	1947–56	18.4
1937–86	10.3	1937–46	4.1
1927–86	9.9	1927–36	7.9
1917–86	9.9	1917–26	9.9
1907–86	9.3	1907–16	5.2

The data in columns 3 and 4 shows the correct way. Look at independent periods: none of the data is overlapping. Each decade is independent. You can see that the figures in the second chart are quite different. Only two are above 10 percent, versus four in the other data. Also, in the independent data two of the eight figures are 5 percent (rounded) or less. None were below 9 percent in the overlapping sample. If you want to know the long-run be-havior—assuming the behavior has not changed—take independent (non-overlapping) samples.

If you want to use the data in the left columns, and you want to use data from 1907, the number to use is 9.3 percent. That's the mean return from 1907 to 1986. It's a much better figure to use than any of the others. If there have not been any structural changes in the market to warrant a more recent figure, then the 9.3 percent figure is the best to use.

If you are not going to use that single figure, then you should proceed as in columns 3 and 4. These contain decade returns for non-overlapping decades.

We can determine the probable error by taking the standard deviation of returns. The probable error of a mean is the standard deviation of the mean divided by the square root of the number of items.

The standard error of the mean is:

standard deviation/$(n-1)^{.5}$

$$= 4.7/(9-1)^{.5}$$
$$= 4.7/2.83$$
$$= 1.7$$

Technically, this means the decade mean should lie between $9.3 - 1.7$ and $9.3 + 1.7$, or between 7.6 and 11.0 two thirds of the time. If you examine the right-hand column, you will see that is not the case. In only three decades was the mean lay between these figures.

Use of non-overlapping decades is a much more reliable means of estimating the mean return from stocks than using overlapping data (and thereby double-counting). Look carefully at the figures if you are evaluating stocks versus bonds, or looking at the record of a mutual fund when that record uses overlapping data.

CHAPTER 16

The Law of the Distribution of Wealth

The dispersion of stock prices has the inevitable consequence that some investors become increasingly wealthy and others become increasingly poor. If 100 investors begin with equal capital and each invests in a different stock, at the end of an hour some will have slightly more than others. At the end of a day, the disparity will be even greater, by the end of a decade the disparity will be pronounced, and after a generation some of the original 100 will be quite rich and others will have lost most of their capital. We assume, of course, that each of the 100 investors kept his money invested in the original stock.

Every stock trader and every investor probably knows or suspects that this dispersion of gains and losses from market action takes place. The dispersion is a cross-sectional dispersion, or dispersion across stocks as some stocks rise in value and others fall. If we take out the mean change in price of all stocks, the market change, we can measure the dispersion across stocks as a function of time. The standard deviation of changes in the logs of value increases with the square root of time (described in Chapter 5).

The dispersion that characterizes the prices of stocks also characterizes the market values, sales and earnings of companies, individual incomes, individual wealth—in fact, a wide range of economic variables.

Yet, coupled with this inevitable dispersion is the other apparently, yet not actually, contradictory fact that each of the 100 investors in the above example has the same probability of percentage increase or decrease as any other investor irrespective of how much his stock has gained or loss in past years or days. If you were the lucky one and gained the most, your chance of a 10 percent gain in the next year is no greater than the chances of other investors at the bottom of the list. Your dollar gain or loss will be greater than theirs because the dispersion is based on log changes, or percentage changes. Your greater wealth will give you greater dollar changes on an equivalent percentage change. This distinction is not easy to describe, but is important to recognize.

What we've just said for stock prices is also true of corporate profits, corporate dividends, corporate assets, and corporate market values. It's true of many other economic variables as well.

How does the process just described affect the ending value of your portfolio, or terminal wealth? In a statistical sense, it is the major determinant of terminal wealth. The result of this kind of dispersion is the skewed distribution of wealth, and the skewed distribution of the market values of corporations. It causes the skewed distribution of the assets, incomes, and dividends of corporations, and of the wealth of individuals. It also partly causes the skewed distribution of the total assets of portfolios managed by trust departments, investment advisors, and mutual funds.

There is more. Not only is the distribution skewed, but it is skewed in a very regular way—a way so regular that it can be described by a law. The law is known as Pareto's law of the distribution of incomes and wealth. In a more general form the law is known as Zip's law—for Zip, a Harvard psychologist, applied it not only to economic factors, but to the distribution of cities by size, newspaper circulation, and to a host of other phenomena.

The law is a variant of the Pareto's distribution of income and wealth. It is:

The cross section distribution of any dollar financial variable becomes increasingly skewed with time and approaches the Pareto distribution.

How does this happen? I first noticed the effect of this rule in looking at the distribution of assets in the customers' stock portfolios. We were interested in reducing the risk in our customer's portfolios. You can reduce the risk in a stock portfolio by increasing the number of stocks, provided you have a nearly equal investment in each. When I started looking at this matter, I assumed that the investments in each stock, while not equal, would have some rough degree of equality. On looking at them, I learned to my surprise that there was very little equality. The distortion was so great, in fact, that a single stock frequently accounted for 50 percent of more of the total value of the portfolio, even in portfolios that had 20 or more stocks. The degree of concentration in a single stock was so great that we measured concentration by counting the number of portfolios with more than half the assets in a single stock.

In searching for reasons for this high degree of concentration—and I'm certain that my bank was no different than any other trust department or money manager—I covered the obvious reasons: the capital gains tax which discouraged sale of stocks with high gains and encouraged sale of stocks with losses; the presence of stocks coming from sale of family companies—stocks that often represented the bulk of the portfolio; reluctance on the part of the portfolio manager or the customer to sell stocks that had done well. These were valid causes of the concentration, but they were not the only causes, or even the major causes. Some local stocks, like Minnesota Mining, were major holdings in many portfolios and they were not stocks that came from family holdings. They had been purchased and rose in value far beyond the others.

The best illustration of the law of the distribution of wealth in the stock market is given by the Fisher and Lorie studies of wealth ratios from the New York Stock Exchange. The data gives wealth ratios at various deciles. Assuming we have one stock at each decile from the 10th to the 90th, we obtain an approximation of how wealth returns become skewed. (The data is taken from the final period (last row) of Fisher and Lorie's Table 3.[1]) First let's look at propoportion of total assets represented by each decile (Table 16.1).

Table 16.1 Estimated Distribution of Assets Represented by Various Stocks After Various Intervals of Time

| Number | Percent of Total Holdings | | |
of Stocks	After 1 Year	After 10 Years	After 40 Years
1	15	20	38
2	13	16	23
3	11	14	16
4	11	12	10
5	10	11	7
6	10	9	4
7	9	8	2
8	9	6	1
9	8	4	—

The largest stock consumes a larger and larger portion of the portfolio. At the start each stock represented 11 percent of the portfolio. After 1 year the largest holding represented 15 percent; after 10 years 20 percent, and after

[1] Fisher, Lawrence and Lorie, James, "Some Studies of Variability of Returns on Common Stocks," *Journal of Business*, 43 (April 1970), 99–134.

40 years 38 percent. The smallest holding declines to 8 percent after a year, 4 percent after 10 years, and less than 1 percent after 40 years. You can see how the portfolio becomes skewed with time. A similar pattern is revealed by the cumulative holdings (Table 16.2).

Table 16.2 Estimated Distribution of Assets Represented by Various Stocks After Various Intervals of Time

	Cumulative Percent of Total Holdings		
Number of Stocks	After 1 Year	After 10 Years	After 40 Years
1	15	20	38
2	28	37	62
3	41	50	77
4	53	62	87
5	63	73	94
6	73	82	98
7	83	89	99
8	62	96	100
9	100	100	100

The dominance of the top stocks increases with time. After 10 years the top 3 stocks have increased their share from 33 percent to 50 percent. By the end of 40 years, they constitute 77 percent of the total value of the portfolio.

The data above represents the actual dispersion of return. We can estimate that dispersion using our market model and the formula for the standard deviation of a log-normal distribution. Let's assume that the standard deviation of changes in the logs of prices is 0.2 and we hold the stocks for 40 years. This gives the distribution shown in Table 16.3.

The simulated results have been estimated using the formula for the standard deviation of the wealth ratio for a log-normal distribution. We assumed the underlying distribution was log-normal. The percentiles were calculated using a normal distribution. The one-year standard deviation for the simulated data was 0.20, which is somewhat lower than the log of the one-year standard deviation/mean (1.55/1.15). Thus, we used the statistics for one year to estimate the wealth distribution after forty years. Notice that the largest stock for the simulation was 36 percent versus 38 percent actual. The second largest holding was 21 percent simulated versus 23 percent actual. The third largest was 14 percent versus 16 percent; fourth and fifth largest were the same, 10 percent versus 10 percent and 7 percent versus 7 percent. Clearly, for the bulk of the portfolio, the simulation gives a quite good prediction of actual—in support of the sixth law.

Table 16.3 Simulated Distribution of Assets Represented by Nine Stocks After Forty Years

Number of Stocks	Percent of Total Holdings		Simulated Cumulative	Actual Cumulative
	Simulated	Actual		
1	36	38	36	38
2	21	23	57	02
3	14	16	70	77
4	10	10	80	87
5	7	7	87	94
6	5	4	92	98
7	4	2	96	99
8	2	1	99	100
9	1	—	100	100

The significance of what we've just said is that you can predict to an approximate degree what your portfolio will look like—in terms of the distribution of holdings—after 40 years if you place equal investments in 9 stocks. There are other implications. It means that we have described the market quite well. The same model will apply to the distribution of sales, or earnings, or assets of corporations.

CHAPTER 17

Diversification Across Time

At a meeting of a pension investment committee, the managing director of the bank trust department that invested the company pension money was explaining why it was important not to try to time the market.

"Between the end of World War II and 1985, an investment of one dollar in common stocks grew to $70.40—provided you kept your money in the market the whole time. But if you had missed the 30 best months of that 40-year period, your one dollar would be worth only $6.11—about the same as your return from T-bills. That is a difference in return of 5 percent versus 12 percent. Therefore," concluded the speaker, "it is extremely dangerous to attempt to time the market—and chance being out at the wrong time."

He went on to explain that stocks compounded at 14 percent over the last decade, but if you had missed 5 of 120 months, your return dropped to 9 percent—a substantial difference.

His point was well taken. I started to calculate the probability of missing those 5 months, but my calculator couldn't handle it. Instead, I decided to examine the data to see whether what he had said made sense. In doing so, I discovered an interesting fact, one which is obvious once you think about it.

The distribution of returns over time is similar to the distribution of returns across stocks. In each case, it is a log-normal distribution. We can calculate the probability of any return. If we form a frequency distribution of returns, say of monthly changes in the logs of price, we will get a distribution that is approximately normal. There will be many small changes—and a few large changes, both positive and negative.

What the bank officer had done was simply to look at the effect on the total return if the high returns were eliminated—if, that is, an investor was out of the market during the months of high returns. Missing the market at certain times has an enormous effect. I suspected that the effect would be similar to the cross-section dispersion of returns on individual stocks in a portfolio with the passage of time. Recall that after a half century, the largest holding accounts for roughly half the total portfolio. I expected a similar effect when looking at the market. I was wrong: it was of an entirely different magnitude—as I soon discovered.

One dollar invested in the S&P 500 Index in 1885 (a century ago) grew to $38.51 by 1985. That works out to an annual compound return of 3.7 percent. If you eliminated the 120 months of highest returns, the overall compound return became negative. You lost money. On the other hand, if you eliminated the 120 worst months, your annual compound return increased from 3.7 to 34 percent per annum—a ninefold increase.

Clearly the impact of the very high and extremely low returns—the tails of the distribution—is great. The impact is much greater on diversification over time than it is on diversification across securities. The reason is that the returns across time are *multiplied* to get the overall return.

In a portfolio, the situation is different. The return on each stock affects that stock's value. The individual stocks are then *added* together to get the new value for the portfolio. The return is calculated from that new sum.

The distinction between added and multiplied is very important. For the market, the effect is multiplicative. For the portfolio, the effect is additive. Even though the underlying mechanism is similar—a log-normal distribution—the effect is entirely different.

In mathematical terms, we can let the variable u represent the return, expressed as first difference in the logs. We can let ut represent the return in a particular month, or year, and us represent the return for a particular security. We then have the following:

Portfolio Return = sum (exp u_s)   (a)

Market Return   = exp (sum u_t)   (b)

Note that formula (a) says sum(exp) while (b) says exp(sum). If we have the two numbers 5 and 5, formula (a) [sum(exp 5,exp 5)]gives us just under 300; formula (b) [exp (5+5)] gives us 22,000. The effect of the two formulas is very different.

Suppose the two variables, u_t and u_i, have the same mean and standard deviation and the same approximately normal distribution. Even though this is so, we have two very different situations. In formula (a)—the portfolio— we have the sum of the exponents. In formula (b)—the market over time— we have the exponent of the sum. For the latter (the market), the tails of the distribution have much greater impact on overall return because the effect is multiplicative, not additive. That point was dramatically made when you saw that by eliminating the 120 worst months in the last century to increase the return *ninefold*.

It is not possible to prepare the same kind of table for diversification over time that we prepared for diversification across securities. That is because the effect is multiplicative, not additive. Each component has a different effect depending on the other components.

However, if you rank returns in descending order and look at the deciles, the effect becomes clear. We did that, converting these to returns to indicate what happens as you select the best months, years, and decades. The results are shown in Table 17.1.

Table 17.1 Annual Compound Return Ranked by Months, Years and Decades Standard & Poor 500 1885–1985

Decile Rank	Ranked by Months	Ranked by Years	Ranked by Decade
1	330	37	10
2	54	17	9
3	33	11	9
4	25	9	6
5	19	7	4
6	15	6	4
7	11	5	1
8	8	4	−1
9	4	2	−1
10	−92	−41	−2

The annual compound returns during the top decile months was 330 percent per year. For the bottom decile months, the return was 92 percent per year. In the best 10 years the average return was 37 percent per year; in the worst 10 it was −41. Choice by decades reduces the range from 10 percent for the top decade to −2 percent for the worst.

The drop in the dispersion of returns by deciles is due to the effect of averaging. The standard deviation of a mean is approximately equal to the mean divided by the square root of the number of items are added. It declines as more items. The annual return has 12 months and the decade return has 120 months. Because you are taking the average of 12 months, or 120 months, instead of one month, the standard deviation declines—and with it the degree of dispersion. This is evident in Table 17.1.

The impact is made even more dramatic if we show what an investment of $1 in each decile would become after a decade, using the deciles of monthly returns, ranked from highest to lowest. The result is given in the Table 17.2. The top decile shows what results from the annual returns on $1 invested for a decade after picking the best 120 months, 10 years, or single decade. The bottom decile shows what results from picking the worst 120 months, 10 years, or single decade.

Table 17.2 Ending Wealth After Ten Years' Investment Ranked by Months, Years and Decade Deciles Standard & Poor 500 1885–1985

Decile Rank	Ranked by Months	Ranked by Years	Ranked by Decades
1	$2,148,423	$23	$2.6
2	73	5	2.4
3	17	3	2.3
4	10	2	1.8
5	6	2	1.5
6	4	2	1.4
7	3	2	1.1
8	2	1	.9
9	2	1	.9
10	.000000000007	.005	.8

An investment of $1 with a return of 330 percent earned during the best months would be worth $2,148,423 at the end of ten years. An investment in the 120 worst months would have reduced your $1 to less than a trillionth of a cent. Your total return over the 100 years would have been $38.52—the product of the amounts in the month column.

If we turn to the ranking by decades, we see that an investment in the best decade of the ten decades would have produced $2.64 after ten years. The worst decade whould have reduced your dollar investment to 84 cents.

As you can see, this table differs greatly from the table showing diversification among various stocks. This is particularly evident in the month column.

To time the market in a way to achieve the most spectacular results would be very difficult, as suggested by the bank officer of our pension investment meeting, because there is a one-in-ten chance of picking the best decade. But the probability of selecting the individual best ten years out of 100 is less than one in ten trillion. The probability of choosing the best—or worst—120 months out of 1201 months would be less than a trillionth of a trillion.

If we had treated diversification over time—using the above data—like diversification over securities, the results would have been quite different. Doing so reveals clearly the difference between the multiplicative effect of time and the additive effect of holding different stocks. We can make the simulation by assuming that we invest $1 each month—or each year, or decade—in the time period in question and then add the amounts together to get a portfolio. (The addition is in contrast with what actually happens when we multiply the results of each time period.)

We can compare the skewness produced by addition with what we obtained above. Using monthly returns, the best 120 months would have produced only 12 percent of the total portfolio. Using decade returns, the best decade of the ten would have amounted to about 17 percent of the total portfolio, roughly the same figure we get with a portfolio of 10 stocks after ten years and a 15 percent standard deviation, which is typical of the market standard deviation.

Clearly, timing the market could produce either spectacular or quite dismal results. Attempting to pick the right time—and being right or wrong—has a far greater effect on return than stock selection. The more pronounced effect is due to the fact that returns over time are *multiplied* together to get the final gain or loss, not added up as in a portfolio.

CHAPTER 18

Predicting Dividend Changes

Dividend income is extremely important to several large classes of investors: individual investors seeking dividend yield; income-oriented trusts; and income-oriented common stock mutual funds. For these investors, the current dividend payment on common stock may not be an accurate measure of future yield because dividends are continually being increased and decreased. Despite the importance of forecasting future changes in dividend payments, there are remarkably few studies of it.

Dividend changes differ in important respects from changes in nearly all other financial variables. For many companies, dividends remain unchanged for long periods, with the same dividend being made year after year. For another, and considerably larger, group of companies, dividend changes are infrequent, less than one change every year or two. For a smaller group of companies, dividend changes are made quite regularly. Yet even in the last group of companies, quarterly payments often remained unchanged for four quarters at a time. The net effect is that the odds of no dividend change are about four in ten, based on a sample of approximately 13,000 dividend changes over 19 years among industrial companies contained in the Compustat tapes.

Compared to changes in dividends, changes in other financial variables occur almost continuously. Earnings per share fluctuate constantly from quarter to quarter and from year to year. It is unusual, rather than common, that earnings are unchanged from one period to the next. Common stock prices shift continuously from day to day, week to week and year to year.

Dividends differ from other financial variables in another respect. Dividend payments can be set by the company directors for most companies in most years. While company directors and company management cannot determine other financial variables, they can establish the current dividend payment within the —limitations imposed by earned income and by any debt covenants. It is this ability to set dividend payments which is largely responsible for the relative constancy of the dividend.

The major uncontrollable restraint is that dividends must generally be paid from current earnings. When earnings fall below the declared dividend, company directors will be forced to consider reducing the dividend. Otherwise, directors are usually reluctant to reduce the existing dividend rate.

The income-oriented investor is generally very concerned with security, in the provision of income and in the continuance of that income. It would be very useful, therefore, to have an accurate model to predict dividend changes, particularly to forecast the probability of dividend increases and reductions.

The most commonly used model, or rule of thumb, is the coverage test. Coverage is computed by dividing earnings available for payment of dividends by the amount of the dividend paid. If earnings per share are $3.00 and the dividend payment is $1.50, coverage is computed by dividing $3.00 by $1.50, which gives a coverage ratio of 2.0 times. Thus, in this example, earnings available are 2.0 times the dividend payment.

Unfortunately, there are several weaknesses in the coverage test. It implicitly assumes a linear relationship between coverage and dividend safety, though the relationship is not linear. In fact, a dividend covered 2.2 times by earnings is four times less likely to be reduced the following year than a dividend covered 1.1 times by earnings.

In order to improve on the coverage ratio, Richard Johnson and I first examined dividend increases and reductions for 900 companies over the period 1948–68.[1] There were 1,750 dividend reductions over that period; of these 1,400 were among stocks where the coverage ratio was in excess of 1.0—i.e., where the dividend payment *was covered* by earnings. The dividend was cut even though earnings *exceeded* dividends. Furthermore, the payment was cut among a group of companies where the overall incidence of reduction in dividends was not high.

Because the simple coverage test as normally used did not provide a systematic measure, we decided to use the reciprocal of the coverage ratio, i.e., the dividend payout ratio to see whether that provided a more systematic relationship to dividend reductions—and also to examine dividend increases. If dividends are $1.50 and earnings are $3.00, the dividend payout ratio is 0.50 or 50 percent.

The results of our study are shown in the Table 18.1, which given the payout ratio and the percent of increases and decreases in dividends.

---

[1] Murphy, J.E. and Johnson, R.S., "Predicting Dividend Changes," *Trusts and Estates*, August 1972, 638–41.

Table 18.1 Payout Ratio and Dividend Reductions, 1949–68

Payout Ratio %	Increase %	Decrease %
10–19	80	6
20–29	79	7
30–39	73	8
40–49	65	10
50–59	48	12
60–69	38	14
70–79	22	20
80–89	17	27
90–99	14	40
100–109	14	44
110–119	6	61
Average	50	13

As you can see, there is a systematic relationship between the payout ratio and the proportion of increases and decreases in the dividend.

For increases there is an inverse relationship between payout and the frequency of increases. The lower the payout, the higher the proportion of increases. This relationship may be stated in terms of the following formula, equating the proportion of decreases to the payout ratio:

Percent of Increases $= 96 - (.84 \times \text{payout})$

For decreases there is a direct relationship when you use the logs of the proportion of increases. In fact, if you plot the proportion of decreases plotted on a log scale against payout on an arithmetic scale you get a nearly straight line. The degree of explanation is very high (r-square = .98). The log of proportion of decreases is a function of payout. The formula for this is:

Percent of Decreases $= e^{1.2 + (.0245 \times \text{payout})}$

Each of the above formulas expresses payout as a percent.

Table 18.1 excludes changes for payouts below 10 percent and above 120 percent where the sample was quite small and the proportion of cuts and increases was no longer a systematic function of payout. The frequency of dividend reduction does not rise when the payout is above 120 percent. Where earnings are negative, the frequency of dividend reduction drops from over 50 percent to 33 percent.

The evidence in the table makes it possible to estimate the probability of a dividend cut next year based on payout last year. Also, you can estimate the probability of a dividend increase from the payout ratio.

Clearly, dividend reduction is a direct function of payout for payout ratios extending from 10 percent to 120 percent, and dividend increase is an inverse function of payout. The direct relationship between payout and dividend reductions makes it possible to forecast the probability of dividend reductions. Similar forecasts can be made for dividend increases.

CHAPTER 19

Basis for Predicting the Probability of Loss

The question of profit or loss is extremely important, to both large and small companies, for instance, mounting losses ultimately drove Penn Central to file for bankruptcy in 1972; banks and investors alike lost hundreds of millions of dollars in defaulted loans and plummeting market values. But losses do not always lead to bankruptcy. More often than not, losses are temporary, particularly among large corporations.

Even these temporary losses have adverse effects. In the years and months preceding a deficit, market declines can be substantial. Credit ratings begin to be adjusted downward, thus hurting bond prices, sometimes severely. The equity shrinks and, with it, the ability to meet coupon or principal payments. The firm's financial structure weakens, and the dividend may be placed in jeopardy. Profitable firms do not normally suffer these disadvantages. Profitable firms can usually make remittances to creditors, meet dividend and coupon payments, repay principal, and retain satisfactory credit ratings.

Despite the importance of the question of future profit or loss, to our knowledge few systematic studies on the prediction of firm profit or loss have been published.

Profits of the firm represent the result of an extremely complex decision-making process involving the exchange of goods and services for money. The participants include members of the firm, suppliers, customers, investors, and lenders. Each exchange usually represents a fair trade of goods and services, or of money, between buyer and seller. The very nature of this process leads one to expect a profit series of differences characterized by a normal distribution, zero mean, and a rate of diffusion or standard deviation which increases with the square root of the differencing or time interval. This is the same process described by the fourth law. The evidence also reveals that successive changes in earnings are uncorrelated, as stated by the second law.

We defined profits by dividing net income by total assets. This measure proved superior to any of 45 other measures of profit in distinguishing future-profit firms from future-loss firms. Using this measure, we created a series of changes in profits found by subtracting from profits in one year profits in the preceding year. We then divided profits in the latest year by the standard deviation of the changes in profits in prior year. This gave us a dimensionless variable, the z-statistic. Having calculated the z-statistic, we can calculate the probability of profit or loss from tables of the normal distribution.

To test the accuracy of the estimates for individual firms, we calculated probabilities of profit and loss for a large number of firms in a given year based on data available in the prior year. Then we classified the firms by estimated probability of loss and compared estimated frequencies with the actual frequencies. The data was taken from the Compustat tapes for the years 1965–76, a total sample of 1,343 firms. The results are shown in Table 19.1.

Table 19.1   Frequency of Loss Among Firms Previously Classified by Probability of Loss

Class in One Year z-score	A	B	C	D	E	F
From	inf	2.4	1.4	1.15	0.55	0.0
To	2.4	1.4	1.15	0.55	0.00	–inf
Loss in next year	48	47	22	48	72	165
Profit next year	4585	639	242	329	297	222
Percent loss	1.1	7.4	9.1	14.7	24.2	43.0

There is a marked correlation between the proportion of realized losses and the z-score. The lower the z-score, the higher the proportion of losses, rising from about 1 percent of all firms with high z-scores to 24 percent of all firms with low scores and 43 percent for negative scores, or firms already unprofitable. Thus, the method effectively groups firms on the basis for future frequency of loss. It is clearly a useful model of estimating the probability that a company will make or lose money in the future. The method is independent of industry; that is, it can be used to compare a bank with a utility, or a retail firm with a chemical firm. That is because this z-score is dimensionless. It is not affected by the particular industry of concern.

CHAPTER 20

How to Read the Probability Tables

The probability tables give probabilities of positive and negative changes for different standard deviations. The standard deviations are given in increments of 5, from 5 to 100. If the standard deviation is not an even multiple of 5, simply take the number closest to the one you are interested in. These should cover most of your needs. The probabilities are given for time intervals of from 1 to 20 years in the future.

The probability tables are given in Appendix II. The tables are based on standard deviations recorded in percent, even though the underlying computation is based on changes in natural logarithms.

In order to use the tables, you first have to determine the standard deviation of the variable you are interested in. Some typical standard deviations follow in Table 20.1, with the numbers given on an annual basis. You can use these if you haven't determined precisely the number you need.

Table 20.1 Annual Standard Deviation

S&P 500 Index 1926–85	
Price	25
Earnings per share	25
Dividends	16
Individual stock price	35
U.S. Interest Rates 1950–86	
1-year bond	40
5-year bond	21
10-year bond	14
20-year bond	12
Consumer Price Index	7

The standard deviation shown in all tables is the 1-year standard deviation, though the tables give probabilities for different numbers of years in the future. Use the 1-year standard deviation to find the appropriate column for every table irrespective of the number of years in the future you are interested in.

For example, if you use a 10-percent standard deviation for 1 year, use the same 10 percent for 2 years or for 20, since the table has made the adjustment in the probabilities for the increased number of years. You needn't do that yourself: it is all provided for you in the tables.

The example of Table II.a, for percent standard deviations, demonstrates how to use the tables (see Table 20.2).

The percent standard deviation is used as follows:

1. Find the table with the forecast period you want, in this case 1 year in the future [1].

2. Locate the appropriate percent, in this case 15 percent [2]. Use this column to see the probabilities for your standard deviation.

3. If you are interested in a particular change, locate that. Here we show a 20 percent increase [3].

4. Find the probability of a change of that much or more, in this case 10 percent. The probability of a 20 percent or greater change one year in the future is 10 percent.

That's the answer: the probability of a 20 percent or greater increase within the next year for a 15 percent standard deviation is 10 percent.

Now for the downside risk. It differs from the upside risk, because the distribution of changes is log normal.

5. Find the percent decline you're interested in. We'll say 20 percent or more [5].

6. Look across to the 15 percent standard deviation column. The probability is 6 percent [6] of a 20 percent or greater drop. That is your downside risk.

If you are interested in 4 years rather than 1, go directly to the 4-year table and proceed as above. Everything is the same, except that you now have different numbers in the 15 percent standard deviation column and in all other columns as well. In 4 years the standard deviation is twice as large. It is increased by the square root of 4. You look to the 15-percent column in Table II.d, since we've adjusted the figures in the columns to take account of the increase in years (see Table 20.3). You may think that the probabilities have increased more than they should, even allowing for the rise in years. What has happened is that the normal probability curve doesn't act as you might think it should—a fact that can be seen by looking at the table for the normal curve given elsewhere in this book. The underlying table is based on natural logarithms.

For a 1-year standard deviation of 15 percent, the probability of a 20 percent increase or more at the end of 4 years is 26 percent. The probability of a 20 percent or more decrease for a 1-year standard deviation of 15 percent after 4 years is 21 percent.

Figure 20.2 (Example of Table II.a) 1 Year In Future [1]

Standard Deviation %

	5	10	15 [2]	20	25	30	35	40	45	50
% Increase Decrease										

Probability of Increase Greater Than Shown

	5	10	15 [2]	20	25	30	35	40	45	50
150	0	0	0	0	0	0	0	0	1	1
100	0	0	0	0	0	1	2	3	3	4
90	0	0	0	0	0	1	2	3	4	6
80	0	0	0	0	0	1	3	4	6	7
70	0	0	0	0	1	2	4	6	8	10
60	0	0	0	0	2	4	6	8	10	12
50	0	0	0	1	3	6	9	11	14	16
40	0	0	1	3	7	10	13	16	18	20
30	0	0	3	8	12	16	19	22	24	26
20[3]	0	3	10 [4]	16	21	24	27	29	31	33
10	3	16	25	30	33	36	38	39	40	41
0	50	50	50	50	50	50	50	50	50	50

Probability of Decrease Greater Than Shown

	5	10	15 [2]	20	25	30	35	40	45	50
0	50	50	50	50	50	50	50	50	50	50
−10	2	13	23	28	32	34	36	38	39	40
−20[5]	0	1	6 [6]	11	16	20	23	25	27	29
−30	0	0	1	3	5	9	12	14	17	19
−40	0	0	0	0	1	3	4	6	8	10
−50	0	0	0	0	0	0	1	2	3	4
−60	0	0	0	0	0	0	0	0	1	1
−70	0	0	0	0	0	0	0	0	0	0
−80	0	0	0	0	0	0	0	0	0	0
−90	0	0	0	0	0	0	0	0	0	0

Figure 20.3 (Example of Table II.d) 4 Years In Future

Standard Deviation %

	5	10	15 [2]	20	25	30	35	40	45	50

% Increase
Decrease

Probability of Increase Greater Than Shown

	5	10	15 [2]	20	25	30	35	40	45	50
150	0	0	0	1	2	4	6	9	11	13
100	0	0	1	3	6	9	12	15	18	20
90	0	0	1	4	8	11	14	17	19	21
80	0	0	2	5	9	13	16	19	21	23
70	0	0	3	7	12	16	19	22	24	26
60	0	1	5	10	15	19	22	24	26	28
50	0	2	7	13	18	22	25	27	29	31
40	0	4	11	18	23	26	29	31	33	34
30	0	8	17	24	28	31	33	35	36	37
20	3	17	26	31	34	36	38	39	40	41
10	16	31	37	40	42	43	44	44	45	45
0	50	50	50	50	50	50	50	50	50	50

Probability of Decrease Greater Than Shown

	5	10	15 [2]	20	25	30	35	40	45	50
0	50	50	50	50	50	50	50	50	50	50
−10	14	29	35	39	41	42	43	44	44	45
−20	1	12	21	27	31	34	36	37	38	39
−30	0	3	10	16	21	25	28	30	32	33
−40	0	0	3	8	13	17	20	22	25	26
−50	0	0	1	3	6	9	12	15	18	20
−60	0	0	0	1	2	4	6	9	11	13
−70	0	0	0	0	0	1	2	4	5	7
−80	0	0	0	0	0	0	0	1	2	2
−90	0	0	0	0	0	0	0	0	0	0

For data that contains negative figures, you will have to estimate the standard deviation using the figures themselves, which for example may be in dollars, or ratios if you have margins. Once you find the standard deviation, express that as a percent of the latest figure, or whatever figure you are interested in.

Say for example that the latest earning figure is $10.00 per share and standard deviation of changes in $5.00, presuming you had to use the dollar figures because some of the past earnings were negative. You obviously couldn't calculate percentage changes, or log changes, for deficits.

Now, $5.00 is 50 percent of the latest figure $10.00. Use the column in the table labeled 50 percent standard deviation. Proceed as above. That's all there is to it.

We could have constructed tables for all kinds of dollar figures, but the above procedure is much easier.

CHAPTER 21

Five Laws of Finance

Some key implications of the random character of stock prices and corporate earnings can be summarized by five laws. The laws permit you to predict the relationship between any two financial variables and to forecast the mean and the variance of the stock market. They are rules of thumb that enable you to evaluate what you hear at a lecture, read in the newspaper or a scholarly article, or are told by you broker, trust officer, or financial adviser. If you are a professional money manager, broker, or analyst, or a student or teacher, the laws will give you a good sense of what to expect in many situations and how to analyze important financial issues. Some of the laws conflict with current theory and practice, and call into question some common methods of analysis and presentation, but they are supported by extensive testing.

The First Law

The first three laws are derived by classifying all financial variables—the numbers you see in the *Wall Street Journal*, in a stock report, or a company annual report—into three types: dollar variables, ratio variables, and percentage change variables.

Dollar variables are variables expressed in dollars. They may be original variables, such as net income or total sales of the corporation, or they may be per share figures, such as the market price of the stock, earnings per share, or dividends per share. Their common characteristic is that there is a dollar sign before them.

Ratio variables are formed by dividing one dollar variable by another. Good examples are the price/earnings ratio, dividend yield, profit margins {net income/sales}, return on equity, and the current ratio. Ratio variables may be recognized by the "sign" or "x" sign that follows them.

Dollar variables and ratio variables behave in the same way. They change slowly and are comparatively stable. If you know last year's sales for General Motors, for example, you can guess fairly well what sales will be

137

this year or next year. The same holds for its return on equity or price-earn-ings ratio. Successive dollar, or ratio, variables are dependent on each other. They are not independent. Table 21.1 provides examples of dollar and ratio variables.

Table 21.1 Dollar and Ratio Variables

Dollar Variables	Ratio Variables
Sales	Sales/Capital
Operating Income	Net Income/Sales
Pretax Income	Payout Ratio
Net Income	Current Ratio
Dividends	Price/Earnings
Current Assets	Debt/Equity
Total Assets	Equity/Total Assets
Long-term Debt	
Sales per Share	
Earnings per Share	
Price	

The first law concerns dollar and ratio variables.

If you correlated sales in the any industry, say by ranking the firms, you would find a high degree of correlation from one year to the next. Why? Con-sider the sales of firms in the chemical industry. A high degree of order characterizes sales of this industry. Sales of DuPont had been at the top for many years, while sales of Rohm & Haas had been at the bottom of this list. The same consistency of sales was found for companies in other industries. If we correlate sales of companies in one year with sales in the next, the coef-ficient of correlation will be positive and high. Table 21.2 shows this.

A variety of factors produce this degree of order. A large company such as DuPont, has a heavy investment in plant, inventory, research and develop-ment, patents and sales and distribution. Its relations with suppliers and cus-tomers are extensive and deep. All these factors combine to produce a continuation of a high volume of sales year after year. Rohm and Haas, on the other hand, has resources which are but a fraction of DuPont's. The ef-fect of the disparity is that the large tend to remain large and the small to remain small. Shifts in rank occur slowly and there is a high degree of cor-relation from one year to the next.

Table 21.2 A Ratio or Dollar Variable in Successive Periods

	Sales 1984*	Rank	1985	Rank
DuPont	35.9	1	29.5	1
Dow	11.4	5	11.5	5
Union Carbide	9.5	2	9.0	2
Monsanto	6.7	3	6.7	3
Celanese	3.3	4	3.0	4
Hercules	2.6	6	2.6	6
Olin	2.1	7	1.8	8
Rohm & Haas	2.0	8	2.1	7

*Sales in billions.

First Law

The values of a dollar or ratio variable of a group of firms in one period will tend to be positively correlated with the values of that same dollar or ratio variable in the next period. The coefficient of correlation will tend to rise as the interval between the periods is decreased.

Extensive tests of the first law are given in the next chapter.

The Second Law

Percentage change variables, the third variable, are formed by taking the percentage change in a dollar variable or a ratio variable. The percent change in a company's stock price, the percent change in earnings per share, the growth of sales, are all percent change variables. Percent change variables have a "%" sign after them. Successive values of a percent change variable are independent; the previous item gives you no idea of what follows.

Table 21.3 provides some examples of percentage change variables.

Table 21.3 Percentage Change Variables

Percent Change in:

Sales	Total Assets
Operating Income	Common Equity
Pretax Income	Earnings per share
Earnings	Dividends per share
Dividends	Price per share

We can illustrate the second law by the example in Table 21.4, where we show percent changes in earnings per share in two independent periods for nine companies in the chemical industry.

Table 21.4 A Percent Change Variable In Two Periods

| | Percent Change in Earnings Per Share | | | |
	83–84	Rank	84–85	Rank
Celanese	77	1	24	1
Union Carbide	70	2	–80	8
Dow Chemical	66	3	–9	2
DuPont	32	4	–14	4
Hercules	31	5	–39	5
Rohm & Haas	26	6	–13	3
Olin	24	7	–54	7
Monsanto	15	8	–49	6

The coefficient of correlation between percent change in the first and the percent change in the second is negative and low, –0.29.

Second Law

The expected coefficient of correlation is zero between the values of a percentage change variable of a group of firms in one period and the values of that same, or any other, percentage change variable in another different period.

The Third Law

The third law is based on an important difference between dollar and ratio variables, on the one hand, and percentage change variables, on the other: percentage change variables are random; dollar and ratio variables are not random.

The third law is derived from this distinction. Remember, the first law stated that the coefficient of correlation between values of a dollar or ratio variable in adjacent periods was high and positive. The second law stated that the expected coefficient of correlation between values of a percentage change variable in adjacent periods was zero. If one kind of variable always results in significantly positive correlation and the other kind always results in zero correlation, then we might expect that the first kind of variable would not be related to the second—that the expected correlation between a dollar or ratio variable and a percentage change variable would be zero. That is the essence of the third law.

Table 21.5 illustrates the law. It shows rates of return on common equity, a ratio variable in 1984, and the percent change in earnings between 1984 and 1985. The results show a correlation not significantly different than zero.

Table 21.5 Return on Common Equity and Change in Earnings Per Share

| | Return | | Change in EPS | |
	1984	Rank	84–85	Rank
Rohm & Haas	17.8	1	−13	3
Celanese	15.3	2	24	1
Hercules	14.7	3	−39	5
Monsanto	12.1	4	−49	6
DuPont	11.6	5	−14	4
Olin	10.0	6	−54	7
Dow Chemical	9.6	7	−9	2
Union Carbide	7.4	8	−80	8

The coefficient of correlation was 0.60 (r^2=.36), but not significantly different from zero.

Third Law

The expected coefficient of correlation is zero between the values of a percentage change variable of a group of firms and the values of a dollar or ratio variable of the same firms.

The Fourth Law

In the chapter on the dispersion of changes in stock prices, we showed how the standard deviation of stock prices rises with the square root of time. That relationship may be stated as a law. It applies to any random variable, though it has been extensively tested only on changes in stock prices, interest rates, the consumer price index, and a few other percentage change variables.

Fourth Law

The volatility (standard deviation of changes) in the stock market rises with the square root of time. The same law applies to other financial variables.

The formula for this relationship is the following:

$$s_k = s_1 k^{.5}$$

The Fifth Law

For a log-normal distribution such as the stock market—and probably most other financial variables—there is an upward bias or positive growth. It arises solely from the statistical nature of the distribution. We covered it in the earlier chapter on the model of the stock market. It may be stated as a law:

$$s(k) = s(1)k^{.5}$$

> Fifth Law

The long-run growth of the stock market is positive even though the odds of a rise or fall are equal. The positive growth is a function of the cross-sectional volatility of the market.

The formula for the fifth law, taken from Chapter 15, is:

$$\text{mean change} = \exp(s^2/2)$$

From a practical standpoint, there is an important result to this law. The result is that there is an upward bias, or growth, to the market. The amount of the bias depends only on the volatility. The more volatile the market, the higher the growth. Table 21.6 shows the compound annual growth in percent for various cross-sectional standard deviations of annual differences in the natural logarithms (see Chapter 15).

Table 21.6 Expected Annual Growth for Various Standard Deviations

Standard Deviation	.10	.15	.20	.25	.30	.35	.40	.45
Compound Growth	0.5	1.1	2.0	3.2	4.6	6.3	8.3	10.7

The second result is that the expected mean annual growth arising from volatility is invariant: it does not rise with the holding period or time interval. It will be the same, no matter how long the period—one year or a hundred. The growth arising from volatility is dependent only on the degree of volatility across the market. When the volatility of the market changes, as it sometimes does, the expected mean long term growth growth arising from that volatility wil also rise.

The expected value, as used in the preceding paragraph, refers to growth arising from volatility determined by the formula for the fifth law (given on page 142) and Table 21.6.

Summary

What do the five laws give us? Above all, some basic knowledge of the whole business of investments, for they provide a way of learning what the expected correlation is between any two financial variables. They tell us which theories are likely to be true and which false. The laws also tell us why the risk of the market—or of any other variable like earnings or dividends—rises with time. And they tell us why the market has an underlying built-in growth—and what it is. Thus the five laws, though they may seem somewhat theoretical, have important practical value: they help us navigate through the choppy seas of conflicting theory and advice that we often receive.

CHAPTER 22

A Summing Up

The goal of this book has been to provide some general concepts which may prove useful in understanding the stock market, and some techniques to use to determine the probability of various outcomes that may be important to your investment decisions.

We have covered some general laws or principles which you may use to determine what is occurring. The first three laws classified all financial variables into different types. The first type was expressed in dollar or ratio terms; the second was expressed as a percentage change. The first type tends to be stable, the second random. Dollar and ratio variables are highly correlated from year to year; percentage change variables do not correlate —their past gives little clue to their future. The essence of this distinction is that you cannot predict future growth from past growth. You cannot predict specific future growth from ratios.

The random nature of the stock market brings with it two different and seemingly contradictory characteristics. Because of randomness, we cannot predict the specific event. We cannot say that Cray Research will rise eight points tomorrow, or that it will be $30 higher at the end of the year. We cannot say that IBM's earnings will rise 10 percent per year each year for the next five years. That kind of predictability is beyond the power of anyone, primarily because there are so many factors that affect future events.

The persistent failure of economists to predict either the direction or magnitude of changes in interest rates any better than the flip of a coin is a well-known illustration of our inability to forecast the specific future event. Their failure is not evidence of lack of knowledge or effort on the part of economists, but simply the intractable nature of the data.

That economists and others continue to make such predictions and that highly sophisticated people continue to accept and act on those predictions, has always been a cause of wonderment. It probably happens because we have a great need for such information. We accept such forecasts, despite our awareness of their fallibility, because we desire them so much and because decisions must be made. But there are other ways of looking at the future.

If the random nature of the underlying data prohibits us from predicting the specific, at the same time it permits us to make other kinds of predictions—predictions deducible from the very random nature of the data. Most of these predictions result from the inherent characteristics of the distribution of changes in the data, from the fact that changes in stock prices are lognormal, from the fact that a lognormal distribution has a positive mean when translated into anti-logs, and from the fact that probabilities may be derived from the normal curve.

This book has attempted to address the practical applications of inherent characteristics of the log-normal distribution. It has focused on the application of those inherent properties in solving practical problems of investment. Just as the inherent properties of the triangle permit the construction of a variety of structures impossible without it, from bridges to office towers, so the lognormal distribution permits estimation of the probability distribution of future values of any variable, estimation of the long-run value of the mean, and calculation of the likely distribution of assets within a common stock portfolio (or the wealth of individuals, or the revenues or profits of corporations), after any interval of time.

Before turning to the applications, we first wish to characterize the distribution. In doing so, we put forth the following principles, or laws:

1. The cross-section correlation between values of a dollar (or ratio) variable in two distinct periods will be positive and high. In other words, the distribution of a variable today—like revenues of companies in the chemical industry, or return on equity—provides a good measure of the distribution of the same variable tomorrow. (First Law.)

2. Past values of a random variable—like percent changes in stock prices, company earnings, or mutual fund performance—won't tell you much about future changes. You can predict neither the magnitude nor the specific direction of a growth variable. (Second Law.)

3. Future values of a random variable—like earnings growth or stock price changes—won't be related to past or current values of a nonrandom variable—like price/earnings ratios, dividend payout, or return on equity. (Third Law.)

4. The distribution of changes in random variables is approximately lognormal—like changes in stock prices, earnings, or price/earnings ratios—so

that you can predict the probability distribution of future changes and there-fore future values.

5. The standard deviation rises with the square root of time. (Fourth Law.)

6. The expected mean change—in stock prices and other variables—over the long run may be determined from the log-normal distribution and the cross-sectional standard deviation. (Fifth Law.)

7. The distribution of wealth—common stock assets in a portfolio, the wealth of individuals, or company sales—becomes skewed in accord with the results of the above laws.

From these principles, or laws, we can derive a number of useful and prac-tical applications.

The first set of estimations come directly from the normal distribution.

The estimates we can make, for example, include the following:

1. We can estimate the probability that stock price of a particular stock will rise by ten percent within the next year, or next decade. Or that the price will fall by ten percent.

2. We can estimate the distribution of price changes of various mag-nitudes.

3. We can determine the probability that a company's profits will rise by 10 percent in the next year, or they will tumble by half.

4. We can find the probability that a company now profitable will lose money next year, or three years from now.

5. We can find the likelihood that a company now in the red will break even next year.

6. We can estimate the probability of a dividend increase.

7. We can determine the probability that our return from a mutual fund over the next 10 years will be 10 percent.

8. We can get a rough estimate of the probability of bankruptcy using the probability of loss as a method of classification, since most companies that go bankrupt are now in red ink, or were.

9. We can estimate the likelihood that profit margins will double.

All of the above estimates are based on the approximation of the normal distribution to the distribution of the variables mentioned, the square root of time rule, and the derivation of a single quantity from the data—the stand-ard deviation.

We can make a second set of estimates from the antilogs of the normal distribution. The most important of these is an estimate of the distribution of assets within a common stock portfolio after a specific interval of time—a year, a decade. An inevitable result of the random nature of changes in stock prices and the normal distribution is not only that portfolios of common stocks become increasingly undiversified with time, but that we can predict the degree of nondiversification—the skew. The growth of undiversification is an inevitable by-product of the log-normal distribution. It is so great as to overpower any reduction in risk by adjusting the portfolio by use of such things as the beta. For the same underlying reason—that is, the random nature of changes in corporate revenues and incomes—we can estimate the future skewing of corporate shares of the revenue and income markets.

Finally, since the distribution of changes in these economic variables is log-normal we can estimate the long-run mean change, which for the stock market is about 5 percent per year.

These are the things we *can* do. The things we *cannot* do are to estimate specific rates of growth based simply on past growth or on ratios. We cannot forecast the returns of a mutual fund based on past returns; we cannot select mutual funds based simply on past returns; we cannot pick the best stock or the best fund in the past and expect it to be the best in the future. There simply isn't enough correlation, or cross-correlation of past and future growth to do that. There are some departures from this: there is some tendency, not very large but quite evident, for low price/earnings portfolios to do better than average over the long run than high price/earnings portfolios, in contradiction of the second law. But this tendency is not sufficiently great to contradict the assertion of the principle that there is generally no significant correlation, or little significant correlation, between that ratio and growth of stock prices.

In conclusion, while it may be heretical to think and propose that all financial variables are random, they are (or seem to be) and that very fact allows us to predict a number of things that are very useful—to an investor, a broker, a corporate official, or anyone interested in the world of stock prices, corporations, and investments.

APPENDIX I

APPENDIX I

Questions on Prediction Answered by the First Three Laws

The first three laws, explained in Chapter 21, can determine whether a given approach is likely to provide a useful prediction. The first seven questions are discussed in detail; the final questions are given in outline form. Most of the questions deal with predicting specific growth rates, rather than probabilities. While probabilities can predicted, specific growth rates are much more difficult to predict. *be*

1. *Can you predict future growth of earnings from past growth of earnings?*

For the vast majority of companies, you cannot because past and future changes are independent. The percent change next year will bear little relation to the percent last year, or in the last decade.

Even relative future growth cannot be predicted from past growth. The company with the best past growth of earnings, say last year's growth, or the past five year's growth, has only an even chance of being above average next year, or in the next five years.

This independence of past and future growth is contrary to what many people think. It means that continuance of "excellence" when measured by earnings growth is not easy to achieve.

Even though you cannot predict the specific rate of growth, you can predict the probability distribution of future earnings changes. Because the volatility of earnings growth varies from one company to the next, the probability distribution will not be the same for all companies.

2. *Can you predict future growth of the price of a company's stock from past growth? Or can you predict future growth of mutual fund from past growth?*

The answer here is the same as with growth of earnings. Successive percentage change variables are independent. The past growth of a stock's price,

153

or a mutual fund's, gives little basis for predicting future growth. Lack of correspondence between past and future holds for absolute growth and for relative growth.

Picking the best stock, or mutual fund, for the future is not easy. You can't simply look at the past growth rate. The extensive records of past mutual fund performance will not help a great deal in choosing the fund with the best future growth. You can tell that because the top funds change from year to year, provided you compare performance for independent years.

But stocks and mutual funds do differ in the volatility. You can use differences in volatility to predict the probable distribution of future percentage changes, though not the specific change.

3. *Can you predict future growth on the basis of return on equity, or share of market?*

Again the answer is no. Percentage change variables are independent and highly variable from year to year. Ratios, such as the return on equity or share of market or profit margins, are comparatively stable from year to year. The two different kinds of variables bear little relation to one another.

Consequently, the company with the highest share of market is not necessarily the company which is likely to show the greatest earnings growth. It may not even have much more than an even chance of doing better than average.

The same conclusion may be drawn about other ratios and growth. High return on equity companies, high profit margin firms, will not show better than average earnings growth, or stock price growth, than companies with low returns or low margins. This conclusion violates commonly held views, but the facts support it.

Certainly there are important advantages to high margins, or high return on equity or high share of market. The advantages include greater ability to pay off debt, remit dividends, finance new activities, and avoid losses or bankruptcy. These advantages should not be minimized. But growth is another matter. The absence of significant correlation between these ratios and growth is due to the comparatively stable behavior of ratios and the much more chaotic behavior of percentage change variables.

4. *Can you predict future share of market, or profit margins, or return on equity, based on past values of these ratios?*

Yes, you can. Ratios, like share of market, or profit margins, change slowly. You can actually predict the probability that a company's margins, or share of market, or profitability, will change from one level to another. You can make the prediction based on the current level of the ratio, the standard deviation of past changes in the ratio, and the normal distribution, as shown in Chapters 12 and 14.

Generally, it is difficult to shift relative position with respect to a ratio or a dollar variable. Just because a firm has low margins doesn't mean it is likely to raise them to the industry norm. In fact, the probability of raising margins may be no better than the probability of lowering them. This phenomenon is related to the calculation of long leads and shifts in leads in the probability theory of fluctuations in coin tossing. In both areas, the most likely event is that relative positions won't shift, but the probability of this drops when relative positions are close together, when the volatility of change rises, and, concurrently, when the time interval rises.

5. Can you predict relative stock price growth on the basis of price/earnings ratios?

In general, no. The assertion that you can violates the law that states that the expected correlation between growth variables and a ratio is zero. If you run correlations between price/earnings ratios at the end of one year and growth of price in the next year, or in the next five years, the coefficients generally will not be significantly different than zero. That makes the odds of prediction low.

Notwithstanding the above, if you classify very large numbers of stocks into a few groups by price/earnings ratios and then examine the average price change for each group, you will find a positive correlation with the average price/earnings ratio for each group. The same conclusion applies to the relation between other growth variables, like earnings, revenues, and ratios.

Doesn't that contradict what we said earlier? Yes and no. It means that for very large groups there is some correlation, but not for individual stocks. There is what we might call weak correlation which comes out in large aggregations over long periods. The correlation may arise from the tendency of the market to overreact. But for stocks individually, there is generally no significant correlation between future price change and past price/earnings ratios.

6. Can you predict future price change if you know future earnings changes?

Yes. There is a significant positive correlation between earnings changes of stocks and coincident price changes. The longer the period of measurement, the greater the correlation. The tests for this were by groups, not large groups, but relatively small groups. This significant relationship confirms the importance of fundamental factors on stock price changes. It may be and seems to be that a stock's price may be only somewhat related to such things as earnings, but the price does respond to changes in earnings on a relative basis.

7. *Can you predict future corporate problems, such as deficits or bankruptcy, from ratios?*

Yes. Firms with low or negative profit margins have a higher incidence of losses and bankruptcy than firms with high margins, or high returns on assets. In examining this relationship, it is preferable to standardize the ratio by dividing it by its standard deviation, as described in Chapter 12. Rarely in the literature or in practice will you find such standardization, but applying it gives you a much better estimate and an estimate from which you can derive a probability.

The following questions show in outline form, but in broader terms, some of the implications of the first three laws. Some questions concern the relation of future changes in a variable to past changes in a variable or to a ratio. Others relate past to future ratios. In all cases where we talk of growth, or changes, we refer to absolute growth, to relative growth, or both, unless otherwise specified. Changes refer to percentage changes.

1. *Is it possible to forecast future changes in the price of a stock using any of the following?*

No it is not.   **Yes it is.**
  (from 2nd law)
Past price change   Concurrent earnings change
Past earnings growth
Past sales growth
  (from 3rd law)
Past price/earnings—very slight only
Past dividend yield
Past return on equity
Past dividend payout ratio

2. Is it possible to forecast future growth of earnings growth using any of the following?

No it is not.
(from 2nd law)
Past earnings growth
Past sales growth
(from 3rd law)
Past return on equity
Present share of market
Past or present earnings retention ratio, relative to other firms

3. Is it possible to forecast of mutual fund performance using any of the following?

No it is not.
(from 2nd law)
Past mutual fund performance

4. Using the corresponding past ratios, is it possible to forecast any of the following future ratios?

> **Yes it is.**
> *(from 1st law)*
> Future share of market
> Future return on equity
> Future price/earnings ratio
> Future dividend/yield
> Future profit margins

APPENDIX II

APPENDIX II

Probability of Various Changes in Standard Deviations at Various Years in the Future

Table II.a   1 Year in Future

	Standard Deviation (%)									
	5	10	15	20	25	30	35	40	45	50
Increase/ Decrease (%)	Probability of Increase Greater Than Shown									
150	0	0	0	0	0	0	0	0	1	1
100	0	0	0	0	0	1	2	3	3	4
90	0	0	0	0	0	1	2	3	4	6
80	0	0	0	0	0	1	3	4	6	7
70	0	0	0	0	1	2	4	6	8	10
60	0	0	0	0	2	4	6	8	10	12
50	0	0	0	1	3	6	9	11	14	16
40	0	0	1	3	7	10	13	16	18	20
30	0	0	3	8	12	16	19	22	24	26
20	0	3	10	16	21	24	27	29	31	33
10	3	16	25	30	33	36	38	39	40	41
0	50	50	50	50	50	50	50	50	50	50
	Probability of Decrease Greater Than Shown									
0	50	50	50	50	50	50	50	50	50	50
−10	2	13	23	28	32	34	36	38	39	40
−20	0	1	6	11	16	20	23	25	27	29
−30	0	0	1	3	5	9	12	14	17	19
−40	0	0	0	0	1	3	4	6	8	10
−50	0	0	0	0	0	0	1	2	3	4
−60	0	0	0	0	0	0	0	0	1	1
−70	0	0	0	0	0	0	0	0	0	0
−80	0	0	0	0	0	0	0	0	0	0
−90	0	0	0	0	0	0	0	0	0	0

Table II.b   2 Years In Future

Increase/Decrease (%)	Standard Deviation (%)									
	5	10	15	20	25	30	35	40	45	50
	Probability of Increase Greater Than Shown									
150	0	0	0	0	0	1	2	3	4	6
100	0	0	0	0	1	3	5	7	9	11
90	0	0	0	1	2	4	7	9	11	13
80	0	0	0	1	3	6	8	11	13	15
70	0	0	0	2	5	8	11	13	16	18
60	0	0	1	3	7	10	13	16	19	21
50	0	0	2	6	10	14	17	20	22	24
40	0	1	4	10	14	18	21	24	26	28
30	0	3	9	15	20	24	27	29	31	32
20	0	9	18	24	28	31	33	35	36	38
10	8	24	31	36	38	40	41	42	43	43
0	50	50	50	50	50	50	50	50	50	50
	Probability of Decrease Greater Than Shown									
0	50	50	50	50	50	50	50	50	50	50
−10	6	22	30	34	37	39	40	41	42	43
−20	0	5	13	19	24	27	30	32	34	35
−30	0	0	4	8	13	17	20	23	25	27
−40	0	0	0	2	5	8	11	14	17	19
−50	0	0	0	0	1	3	5	7	9	11
−60	0	0	0	0	0	1	2	3	4	6
−70	0	0	0	0	0	0	0	1	1	2
−80	0	0	0	0	0	0	0	0	0	0
−90	0	0	0	0	0	0	0	0	0	0

Table II.c   3 Years in Future

	Standard Deviation (%)									
	5	10	15	20	25	30	35	40	45	50
Increase/ Decrease (%)			*Probability of Increase Greater Than Shown*							
150	0	0	0	0	1	2	4	6	8	10
100	0	0	0	1	4	6	9	12	14	16
90	0	0	0	2	5	8	11	14	16	18
80	0	0	1	3	6	10	13	16	18	20
70	0	0	1	5	8	12	15	18	20	22
60	0	0	3	7	11	15	18	21	23	25
50	0	1	5	10	15	19	22	24	26	28
40	0	2	8	14	19	23	26	28	30	32
30	0	6	14	20	25	28	31	33	34	35
20	2	13	23	28	32	34	36	38	39	40
10	13	28	35	38	40	42	43	44	44	45
0	50	50	50	50	50	50	50	50	50	50
			Probability of Decrease Greater Than Shown							
0	50	50	50	50	50	50	50	50	50	50
−10	11	26	33	37	39	41	42	43	43	44
−20	0	9	18	24	28	31	33	35	36	38
−30	0	2	7	13	18	22	25	27	29	31
−40	0	0	2	5	9	13	16	19	21	23
−50	0	0	0	1	4	6	9	12	14	16
−60	0	0	0	0	1	2	4	6	8	10
−70	0	0	0	0	0	0	1	2	3	4
−80	0	0	0	0	0	0	0	0	1	1
−90	0	0	0	0	0	0	0	0	0	0

Table II.d   4 Years In Future

	Standard Deviation (%)									
	5	10	15	20	25	30	35	40	45	50
Increase/ Decrease (%)			Probability of Increase Greater Than Shown							
150	0	0	0	1	2	4	6	9	11	13
100	0	0	1	3	6	9	12	15	18	20
90	0	0	1	4	8	11	14	17	19	21
80	0	0	2	5	9	13	16	19	21	23
70	0	0	3	7	12	16	19	22	24	26
60	0	1	5	10	15	19	22	24	26	28
50	0	2	7	13	18	22	25	27	29	31
40	0	4	11	18	23	26	29	31	33	34
30	0	8	17	24	28	31	33	35	36	37
20	3	17	26	31	34	36	38	39	40	41
10	16	31	37	40	42	43	44	44	45	45
0	50	50	50	50	50	50	50	50	50	50
			Probability of Decrease Greater Than Shown							
0	50	50	50	50	50	50	50	50	50	50
−10	14	29	35	39	41	42	43	44	44	45
−20	1	12	21	27	31	34	36	37	38	39
−30	0	3	10	16	21	25	28	30	32	33
−40	0	0	3	8	13	17	20	22	25	26
−50	0	0	1	3	6	9	12	15	18	20
−60	0	0	0	1	2	4	6	9	11	13
−70	0	0	0	0	0	1	2	4	5	7
−80	0	0	0	0	0	0	0	1	2	2
−90	0	0	0	0	0	0	0	0	0	0

Table II.e   5 Years In Future

Increase/ Decrease (%)	Standard Deviation (%)									
	5	10	15	20	25	30	35	40	45	50
	Probability of Increase Greater Than Shown									
150	0	0	0	1	3	6	9	11	14	16
100	0	0	1	4	8	12	15	18	20	22
90	0	0	2	6	10	14	17	20	22	24
80	0	0	3	7	12	16	19	22	24	26
70	0	1	4	10	14	18	21	24	26	28
60	0	1	7	12	17	21	24	27	29	30
50	0	3	10	16	21	24	27	29	31	33
40	0	6	14	20	25	28	31	33	34	36
30	1	11	20	26	30	33	35	36	38	39
20	5	20	28	33	36	38	39	40	41	42
10	19	33	38	41	42	44	44	45	45	46
0	50	50	50	50	50	50	50	50	50	50
	Probability of Decrease Greater Than Shown									
0	50	50	50	50	50	50	50	50	50	50
−10	17	31	37	40	42	43	44	44	45	45
−20	2	15	24	29	33	35	37	38	39	40
−30	0	5	13	19	24	27	30	32	33	35
−40	0	1	5	11	15	19	22	25	27	29
−50	0	0	1	4	8	12	15	18	20	22
−60	0	0	0	1	3	6	9	11	14	16
−70	0	0	0	0	1	2	4	5	7	9
−80	0	0	0	0	0	0	1	2	3	4
−90	0	0	0	0	0	0	0	0	0	1

Table II.f   10 Years In Future

	Standard Deviation (%)									
	5	10	15	20	25	30	35	40	45	50
Increase/ Decrease (%)			Probability of Increase Greater Than Shown							
150	0	0	2	6	10	13	17	19	22	24
100	0	1	6	11	16	20	23	26	28	29
90	0	2	7	13	18	22	25	27	29	31
80	0	3	9	15	20	24	27	29	31	32
70	0	4	11	18	23	26	29	31	33	34
60	0	6	14	21	25	29	31	33	34	36
50	0	9	18	24	28	31	33	35	37	38
40	1	13	22	28	32	34	36	38	39	40
30	4	19	28	32	36	38	39	40	41	42
20	12	27	34	38	40	41	42	43	44	44
10	27	38	41	43	45	45	46	46	47	47
0	50	50	50	50	50	50	50	50	50	50
			Probability of Decrease Greater Than Shown							
0	50	50	50	50	50	50	50	50	50	50
−10	25	36	41	43	44	45	46	46	46	47
−20	7	23	31	35	38	39	41	42	42	43
−30	1	12	21	27	31	33	35	37	38	39
−40	0	5	12	19	23	27	30	32	33	35
−50	0	1	6	11	16	20	23	26	28	29
−60	0	0	2	6	10	13	17	19	22	24
−70	0	0	0	2	4	7	10	13	15	17
−80	0	0	0	0	1	3	4	7	9	10
−90	0	0	0	0	0	0	1	2	3	4

Table II.g   15 Years In Future

	Standard Deviation (%)									
	5	10	15	20	25	30	35	40	45	50
Increase/ Decrease (%)			Probability of Increase Greater Than Shown							
150	0	1	5	10	14	18	22	24	26	28
100	0	3	10	16	21	25	28	30	32	33
90	0	4	12	18	23	26	29	31	33	34
80	0	6	14	20	25	28	31	33	34	35
70	0	8	16	23	27	30	32	34	36	37
60	1	10	19	25	29	32	34	36	37	38
50	2	14	23	28	32	34	36	38	39	40
40	4	18	27	32	35	37	39	40	41	42
30	2	24	31	36	38	40	41	42	43	43
20	17	31	37	40	42	43	44	44	45	45
10	31	40	43	45	46	46	47	47	47	48
0	50	50	50	50	50	50	50	50	50	50
			Probability of Decrease Greater Than Shown							
0	50	50	50	50	50	50	50	50	50	50
−10	29	39	42	44	45	46	46	47	47	47
−20	12	27	34	38	40	41	42	43	44	44
−30	3	17	25	31	34	36	38	39	40	41
−40	0	8	17	23	28	31	33	35	36	37
−50	0	3	10	16	21	25	28	30	32	33
−60	0	1	5	10	14	18	22	24	26	28
−70	0	0	1	4	8	12	15	18	20	22
−80	0	0	0	1	3	6	8	11	13	15
−90	0	0	0	0	0	1	2	4	5	7

Table II.h   20 Years In Future

Increase/Decrease (%)	Standard Deviation (%)									
	5	10	15	20	25	30	35	40	45	50
	Probability of Increase Greater Than Shown									
150	0	2	7	13	18	22	25	27	29	31
100	0	5	13	20	24	28	30	32	34	35
90	0	7	15	22	26	29	32	33	35	36
80	0	8	17	24	28	31	33	35	36	37
70	1	11	20	26	30	33	35	36	37	38
60	2	14	23	28	32	34	36	38	39	40
50	3	17	26	31	34	36	38	39	40	41
40	6	21	30	34	37	39	40	41	42	43
30	11	27	34	37	40	41	42	43	44	44
20	20	33	39	41	43	44	45	45	46	46
10	33	41	44	45	46	47	47	47	48	48
0	50	50	50	50	50	50	50	50	50	50
	Probability of Decrease Greater Than Shown									
0	50	50	50	50	50	50	50	50	50	50
−10	31	40	43	45	46	46	47	47	47	48
−20	15	30	36	39	41	42	43	44	45	45
−30	5	20	28	33	36	38	40	41	42	42
−40	1	12	21	27	30	33	35	37	38	39
−50	0	5	13	50	24	28	30	32	34	35
−60	0	2	7	13	18	22	25	27	29	31
−70	0	0	3	7	11	15	18	21	23	25
−80	0	0	1	2	5	9	12	14	17	19
−90	0	0	0	0	1	2	4	6	8	10

APPENDIX III

APPENDIX III

Distribution of Common Stock Assets Among Different Stocks in Subsequent Years for Different Standard Deviations as a Result of the Log-Normal Distribution

Table III.a

	Standard Deviation 15%								
	Number of Years Later								
	0	1	2	5	10	20	30	40	50
Number of Stocks	Percent in Each Stock								
1	11	13	14	16	18	22	25	28	30
2	11	12	13	14	15	17	18	19	19
3	11	12	12	13	13	14	14	14	14
4	11	11	12	12	12	12	11	11	11
5	11	11	11	11	10	10	9	9	9
6	11	11	10	10	9	8	8	7	7
7	11	10	10	9	8	7	6	6	6
8	11	10	9	8	7	6	5	4	4
9	11	9	8	7	6	4	4	3	2

	Standard Deviation 20%								
	Number of Years Later								
	0	1	2	5	10	20	30	40	50
Number of Stocks	Percent in Each Stock								
1	11	14	15	18	21	26	30	33	37
2	11	13	14	15	16	18	19	20	21
3	11	12	12	13	14	14	14	14	14
4	11	12	12	12	12	11	11	10	10
5	11	11	11	11	10	9	8	8	7
6	11	11	10	10	9	7	6	6	5
7	11	10	10	9	7	6	5	4	4
8	11	9	9	8	6	5	4	3	2
9	11	9	8	6	5	3	2	2	1

171

Standard Deviation 25%
Number of Years Later

Number of Stocks	0	1	2	5	10	20	30	40	50
				Percent in Each Stock					
1	11	15	16	20	24	30	35	39	43
2	11	13	14	16	17	19	20	21	21
3	11	12	13	13	14	14	14	13	13
4	11	12	12	12	11	11	10	9	8
5	11	11	11	10	10	8	7	6	6
6	11	10	10	9	8	6	5	4	4
7	11	10	9	8	7	5	4	3	2
8	11	9	8	7	5	4	3	2	2
9	11	8	7	5	4	2	2	1	1

Standard Deviation 30%
Number of Years Later

Number of Stocks	0	1	2	5	10	20	30	40	50
				Percent in Each Stock					
1	11	15	17	21	26	34	40	45	49
2	11	14	15	16	18	20	21	22	22
3	11	12	13	14	14	14	13	13	12
4	11	12	12	12	11	10	9	8	7
5	11	11	11	10	9	8	6	5	5
6	11	10	10	9	7	6	4	3	3
7	11	9	9	7	6	4	3	2	2
8	11	9	8	6	5	3	2	1	1
9	11	8	7	5	3	2	1	1	0

Table III.b

Standard Deviation 15%
Number of Years Later

Number of Stocks	0	1	2	5	10	20	30	40	50
				Cumulative Percent					
1	11	13	14	16	18	22	25	28	30
2	22	26	27	30	34	39	43	46	49
3	33	38	39	43	47	53	57	60	63
4	44	49	51	55	59	64	68	71	74
5	56	60	62	65	69	74	78	80	82
6	67	71	72	75	79	83	85	87	89
7	78	81	82	84	87	90	92	93	94
8	89	91	91	93	94	96	96	97	98
9	100	100	100	100	100	100	100	100	100

Standard Deviation 20%
Number of Years Later

Number of Stocks	0	1	2	5	10	20	30	40	50
					Cumulative Percent				
1	11	14	15	18	21	26	30	33	37
2	22	27	29	33	37	44	49	54	57
3	33	39	41	46	51	58	64	68	71
4	44	50	53	58	63	70	74	78	81
5	56	61	64	68	73	79	83	85	88
6	67	72	74	78	82	86	89	81	93
7	78	82	83	86	89	93	94	95	96
8	89	91	92	94	95	97	98	98	99
9	100	100	100	100	100	100	100	100	100

Standard Deviation 25%
Number of Years Later

Number of Stocks	0	1	2	5	10	20	30	40	50
					Cumulative Percent				
1	11	15	16	20	24	30	35	39	43
2	22	28	30	35	41	49	55	60	64
3	33	40	43	49	55	64	69	74	77
4	44	52	55	60	67	74	79	83	86
5	56	63	65	71	76	83	87	89	91
6	67	73	75	80	84	89	92	94	95
7	78	83	85	88	91	94	96	97	98
8	89	82	93	95	96	98	98	99	99
9	100	100	100	100	100	100	100	100	100

Standard Deviation 30%
Number of Years Later

Number of Stocks	0	1	2	5	10	20	30	40	50
					Cumulative Percent				
1	44	15	17	21	26	34	40	45	49
2	22	29	32	38	45	54	61	66	70
3	33	41	45	51	59	68	74	79	82
4	44	53	56	63	70	78	83	87	90
5	56	64	67	73	79	86	90	92	94
6	67	74	77	82	86	91	94	96	97
7	78	83	86	89	92	96	97	98	99
8	89	92	93	95	97	98	99	99	100
9	100	100	100	100	100	100	100	100	100

APPENDIX IV

APPENDIX IV

How to Find the Probability from the Z-Score

In statistics we often show deviations from the mean by measuring them off in units of the standard deviation—often called z-score (or z-value). Using the z-value, we can compare two different distributions. We can also compare values from two different variables. If the distribution is normal, we can tell what proportion of the observations fall above or below or between various values of the variable.

Any value in a distribution can be converted into a z-value by subtracting the mean of the distribution and dividing the difference by the standard deviation. For example, when the mean is 60 and the standard deviation is 10, a raw score of 70 would have a z-value of $(70 - 60)/10 = 10/10 = 1$. That means, 1 standard deviation above the mean = a z-value (or z-score) of 1.

Table IV.a   Tables for Finding Probability of Loss from Z-Score

Positive Earnings	
Earnings/Standard Deviation of Changes in Earnings z-score	Probability of Loss (%)
.00	50%
.05	48
.10	46
.15	44
.20	42
.25	40
.30	38
.35	36
.40	34
.50	31
.60	27
.70	24
.80	21
.90	18

Positive Earnings (continued)

Earnings/Standard Deviation of Changes in Earnings z-score	Probability of Loss (%)
1.00	16
1.10	14
1.20	11
1.30	10
1.40	8
1.50	7
1.60	6
1.70	5
1.80	4
1.90	3
2.00	2
2.25	1

Negative Earnings

Earnings/Standard Deviation of Changes in Earnings z-score	Probability of Loss (%)
.00	50%
.05	52
.10	54
.15	56
.20	58
.25	60
.30	62
.35	64
.40	66
.50	69
.60	73
.70	76
.80	79
.90	82
1.00	84
1.10	86
1.20	88
1.30	90
1.40	92
1.50	93
1.60	95
1.70	96

Negative Earnings (continued)

Earnings/Standard Deviation of Changes in Earnings z-score	Probability of Loss (%)
1.80	96
1.90	97
2.00	98
2.25	99

Table IV.b   Table for Finding Probability of Change in Value

Z-Score Change in Value/ Standard Deviation of Change	Probability of Change (%)
.00	50%
.05	48
.10	46
.15	44
.20	42
.25	40
.30	38
.35	36
.40	34
.50	31
.60	27
.70	24
.80	21
.90	18
1.00	16
1.10	14
1.20	11
1.30	10
1.40	8
1.50	7
1.60	6
1.70	5
1.80	4
1.90	3
2.00	2
2.25	1

APPENDIX V

Testing the First Three Laws of Financial Relationships

In order to test the first three laws, Russ Nelson and I ran extensive correlations on dollar, ratio, and percentage change variables for twelve industries. The initial tests were reported in the *Financial Analysts Journal*; later, tests were presented at the annual meeting of the Western Finance Association and in the *Journal of Quantitative and Financial Analysis*.

Recall that the first law concerned dollar or ratio variables for a group of firms in two periods—cross-sectional correlation.

First Law

The values of a dollar or ratio variable of a group of firms in one period will tend to be positively correlated with the values of that same dollar or ratio variable in the next period. The coefficient of correlation will tend to rise as the interval between the periods is decreased.

In order to test the first law, we compared dollar and ratio variables for 19 firms in the petroleum industry, 24 companies in the chemical industry, and 22 companies in the metals industry. The data was taken from the Compustat annual industrial tape> over the 18 years 1949–67 for 12 variables. The dollar variables were revenues, pretax income, cash flow, earnings, price, dividends; the ratio variables were price/earnings, dividend yield, earnings/equity, pretax profit margins, common equity/total assets and dividend payment. To insure compatibility, only companies that consistently reported on a calendar year basis were included in the sample. All tests on this sample were run using single-year periods; the sample included only companies with a full 18 years of data for all 12 variables.

Because of the large number of coefficients of correlation—over 65,000—we show the frequency distributions of the coefficients for the

183

petroleum industry. Although the tests were restricted to the larger firms of a few industries for selected periods, the consistency of the results suggests that the same results apply to other samples of firms, other length periods, and other years.

The frequency distribution of the 192 coefficients for tests of the first law of the petroleum industry is shown in Table V.a.

Table V.a   Distribution of Correlation Coefficients of Dollar and Ratio Variables of 19 Petroleum Firms—Adjacent Years

From	−1.0	−.8	−.6	−.4	−.2	0	.2	.4	.6	.8
To	−.6	−.6	−.4	−.2	0	.2	.4	.6	.8	1.0
Percent	0	0	0	0	0	0	0	1	4	95

As you can see, all of the coefficients were positive, all were above +.4 and 95 percent were above +.8. Since for this sample, a coefficient of +.44 is significant at the .05 level of significance, all of the coefficients were significantly positive.

Second Law

The expected coefficient of correlation is zero between the values of a percentage change variable of a group of firms in one period and the values of that same, or any other, percentage change variable in another different period.

The original evidence for the second law was that extensive evidence confirms that changes in stock prices approximate a random walk. The next piece of evidence came from the work on the randomness of changes in earnings. The model of a random walk appears to apply to changes in other financial variables. If changes are random, past changes give no information about future changes. Consequently, a firm's relative growth of any variable in one year will give little clue as to its relative growth in any other year, or to the relative growth of any other variable in any succeeding or preceding year.

Note that the laws specifically says the lack of relationship applies to variables in different periods, not the same period.

Considerable evidence has been presented in the literature on the lack of correlation of past and future percentage changes of stock prices and earnings per share. This evidence supports the second law for those two variables.

Extensive tests were done on 65 companies in the petroleum, chemical, and metals industries. Based on various combinations of one year periods, varying lags over the years 1951–67, and percentage changes in the variables described above, 10,608 coefficients of correlation were computed. The frequency distribution of those coefficients in shown in Table V.b.

Table V.b   Distribution of Correlation Coefficients of Pairs of Various Percentage Change Variables in Distinct Periods and for Varying Intervals Between Periods for 19 Firms in the Petroleum Industry

From	−1.0	−.8	−.6	−.4	−.2	0	.2	.4	.6	.8
To	−.6	−.6	−.4	−.2	0	.2	.4	.6	.8	1.0
Number	4	67	623	1694	3002	2878	1685	563	85	7
Percent	0	1	6	16	28	27	16	5	1	0

The average coefficient of correlation is approximately zero; 55 percent of the coefficients lie between −.2 and +.2. The proportion that are either significantly positive (greater than +.44) or significantly negative (less than −.44) was approximately 10 percent, the amount that would be expected using a two-tailed test and a level of significance of 5%. Similar results were obtained in the chemical and metal industries.

Third Law

The expected coefficient of correlation is zero between the values of a percentage change variable of a group of firms and the values of a dollar or ratio variable of the same firms.

The third law concerns the correlation between a dollar or ratio variable and a percentage change variable.

To investigate the third law in detail, we used the variables described previously. Coefficients of correlation were computed between the values of a percentage change variable and the values of a dollar or ratio variable. Different combinations were examined as were different intervals of time between test years. This resulted in 10,608 coefficients of correlation. The frequency distribution of these coefficients for the petroleum industry is given in Table V.c.

Table V.c   Distribution of Correlation Coefficients of Pairs of Various Dollar or Ratio with Percentage Change Variables for Varying Intervals Between Periods for 19 Firms in the Petroleum Industry

From	−1.0	−.8	−.6	−.4	−.2	0	.2	.4	.6	.8
To	−.6	−.6	−.4	−.2	0	.2	.4	.6	.8	1.0
Number	1	132	558	1469	2684	3018	1970	680	55	0
Percent	0	1	5	14	25	28	19	6	1	0

The table affirms the hypothesis. The mean coefficient of correlation is approximately zero. Fifty-three percent of the coefficients fall between −.2 and +.2, or very low. The proportion of coefficients that are either significantly positive or significantly negative is roughly 10 percent, the proportion to be expected from a random selection from a population that approaches normality and has a mean coefficient of zero. Similar results were obtained in the study of the chemical and metals industries.

The evidence for the third law, like the evidence for the first two laws, confirms it. The three laws suggest that if you want to estimate future growth, you can't just extrapolate from past growth or from some ratios. The financial world is simply too complex, too complicated, too subject to a wide variety of influences for that. The laws are guidelines—by remembering them you can generally determine whether a relationship between two or more variables may be presumed to exist, or not.

APPENDIX VI

The Effect of the Holding Period, or Time, on Dispersion

One of the most important characteristics of a random series is that the dispersion of the series rises with the square root of time. If we take the standard deviation as our measure of dispersion, we will find that it rises with the square root of the holding period. The standard deviation is a general measure of volatility, and as such its tendency to rise with the square root of time reveals that volatility rises with time.

To cite specific examples, the degree of change in changes in stock prices, measured by the standard deviation, rises with the square root of the holding period. This is shown in the following example, in which the standard deviation of annual changes in stock prices is 18%. To obtain the standard deviation of changes for any other number of years, multiply the 1-year standard deviation by the square root of the number of years.

Standard deviation for n years

$$= \text{1-year standard deviation} \times \text{(number of years)}^{.5}$$

Taking the 1-year standard deviation as 18 percent, we obtain the following figures for standard deviations for from 2 to 10 years:

Number of years	Years^5 × 18%=	Standard Deviation for n years
1	1 × 18% =	18%
2	1.41 × 18 =	25
3	1.73 × 18 =	31
4	2 × 18 =	36
5	2.24 × 18 =	40
6	2.45 × 18 =	44
7	2.65 × 18 =	48
8	2.83 × 18 =	51
9	3 × 18 =	54
10	3.16 × 18 =	57

If you know the standard deviation for 1-year changes in stock prices, or say in the Dow Jones Industrial Average, you can calculate the standard deviation for any other number of years using the above formula. The formula is not perfect—it is approximate, but it is sufficiently accurate to be useful.

When we plot a relationship such as the square root rule shown above on log-log paper, we get a straight line with a slope of one-half. The one-half corresponds to the t^5 rule. The rise in the standard deviation is always half the run; the change in the value of the change in y is exactly half the value of the change in x. We can show that in the first panel of Figure VI-1 which gives the standard deviation versus the time interval for the data given above. This plot and all the others are on a log-log scale.

The first panel of Figure VI-1 is an ideal figure in which the relationship is perfect. In practice we will obtain only an approximate figure. The slope, rather than being 0.5, may range as high as 0.6 or as low as 0.4, or even wider afield, and the dots will not lie on a perfectly straight line. To demonstrate the degree of approximation, we provide figures for selected random, stock market, corporate earnings and revenues, consumer price index, and interest rate data. In each case we use overlapping intervals, which tend to smooth the data somewhat. For both overlapping and nonoverlapping data, the fit of a regression line is significant at the 5-percent level of significance, which means that the relationship is not due to chance, but real.

The second panel of Figure VI-1 is for a set of random data. You can see that the slope is very close to one-half, the square root rule. The actual slope is 0.5

The third panel gives the standard deviation of changes in the natural logarithm of stock prices versus the differencing interval. The data is for the S&P 500 Index for the years 1926–85. The slope is 0.5. More extensive examples are given in Osborne (1957), who provides data both for sequential data and cross-sectional data. Both kinds of data have a slope of approximately 0.5.

The fourth panel is for earnings of the S&P 500 over the same period. The y-axis gives the standard deviation of changes in the natural logarithm of earnings and the x-axis gives the time (difference) interval. The slope is slightly more than 0.5.

The fifth panel covers S & P 500 Dividends, the standard deviation of changes in the natural logarithm of dividends on the y-axis versus the

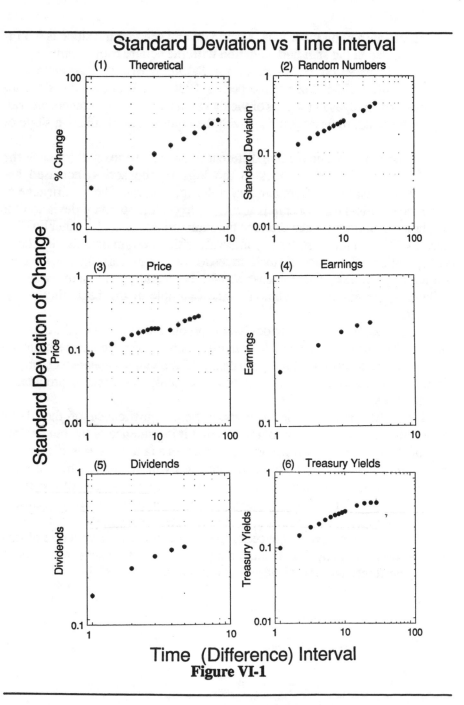

Figure VI-1

difference interval on the x-axis. Again you can see that the slope is 0.5 indicating a rise in the standard deviation with the square root of time.

The sixth panel covers yields on the Salomon Brothers 3-Month U.S. Treasury bill yield index for the period 1950–86. It shows the standard deviation of changes in the logs of yields versus the time difference interval. Again the standard deviation rises with the square root of time—a slope of 0.5.

The above figures cover five different economic series and for each the standard deviation of changes in the logs of the series increased approximately with the differencing, or holding, interval. The significance of this mathematical relationship is that if we know the standard deviation for one holding period, we can estimate the standard deviation for other holding periods. We can forecast, for any interval, within certain bounds, the standard deviation of changes in stock prices, or corporate earnings, or the consumer price index. The forecast should be made in the same way we calculated the standard deviation in the example at the beginning of the chapter.

Once we know the standard deviation and once we know that the distribution of changes reflects a well known distribution, like the normal distribution, then we can forecast the probability of a change greater than, or less than, any magnitude. We have the power to make forecasts of probability distributions.

That's the practical use. The theoretical significance of the above demonstration of the square root rule is that it is evidence of the random nature of changes in the above economic series. In a random series, dispersion, measured by the standard deviation, increases with the square root of time. In a nonrandom series that is not the case. The fact that each of the above series has a standard deviation that increases with the square root of time is evidence that they behave like a random series, like a random walk. That being the case, we have evidence for the application of the structure of random series to making statements about the future, forecasts, about stock prices, earnings, and other investment variables.

APPENDIX VII

Formulas

Let $x_{j,t}$ represent the value of a dollar or ratio variable for the j_{th} firm ($j=1,2,...,n$) at time t ($t=1,2,...,n$). Furthermore, let

$$X_t = [x_{1,t}, x_{2,t},..., x_{n,t}] \text{ and}$$

$$X_{t+k} = [x_{1,t+k}, x_{2,t+k},..., x_{n,t+k}]$$

where X_t represents the values of a dollar or ratio variable for m firms at time t and X_{t+k} represents the values of this same variable for the same group of firms at time t+k. To illustrate, X_t might represent earnings of firms in the chemical industry in 1986 and X_{t+k} might represent earnings of the same firms in 1987. The first law states:

$$E \, cor \, (X_t, X_{t+k}) \rightarrow 1 \text{ as } k \rightarrow 0 \tag{1}$$

where "E cor" stands for the expected coefficient of correlation. The first law states that the expected value of the coefficient of correlation between X_t and X_{t+k} tends to 1 as k tends to 0. As the value of k departs from zero, the absolute value of the coefficient may be expected to decline from 1.

Next, let

$$\Delta vx_{j,t} = 100(x_{j,t} - x_{j,t-k})/ \, x_{j,t-k}$$

where Δvx_{jt} represents the percent change in a dollar or ratio variable of the j_{th} firm between period t–k and period t.

Furthermore, let

$$\Delta X_t = [x_{1,t}, \, x_{2,t},..., \, x_{n,t}]$$

and

$$\Delta Y_{t+k} = [y_{1,t+k}, \, y_{2,t+k},..., \, y_{n,t+k}]$$

where ΔX_t represents the values of a percentage change variable in period t and $\Delta v Y_{t+k}$ represents the values of the same, or a different, percentage change variable in period t+k. For example, ΔvX_t and ΔvY_{t+k} might represent percentage changes in sales of firms in the chemical industry in 1986 and 1987, respectively.

195

Then, the second law states:

$$E \, cor(\Delta v X_t, \Delta v Y_{t+k}) = 0 \qquad (2)$$

where $k \neq 0$ and $X = Y$ or $X \neq Y$

Equation (2) states that the expected coefficient of correlation is zero between a percentage change variable (X_t) in one period and the same, or any other, percentage change variable $(\Delta v Y_{t+k})$ in another different period. From equations (1) and (2), it is possbile to infer a third law, namely:

$$E \, cor \, (X_t, \Delta v Y_{t+k}) = 0 \text{ where } X = Y \text{ or } X \neq Y \qquad (3)$$

where k may or may not equal zero and X_t and $\Delta v Y_{t+k}$ may or may not be the same variable.

Equation (3) states that the expected coefficient of correlation between a dollar or ratio variable (X_t) and a percentage change variable $(\Delta v Y_{t+k})$ is zero.

We have defined a percentage change variable as $100 \, (y_t - y_{t-k})/y_{t-k})$. The equations apply equally well if we use, instead of the percentage change, the first difference in the natural logarithms—$\ln(y_t) - \ln(y_{t-k})$. For changes of under 15%, the first difference in the natural logs is nearly the same as the percentage change, i.e., a percentage change of 10% is the same as the difference in the natural logs of 0.10.

If first differences in the natural logarithms are approximately normally distributed, with a standard deviation σ, and if σ is approximately stable over time, then it is a fact that σ will increase with the square root of time. Letting σ represent the standard deviation and

$$u_t = \ln(y_t) - \ln(y_{t-k})$$

over the time interval k.

Then,

$$\sigma_k = \sigma_1 k^5 \qquad (4)$$

Equation (4) means that if the standard deviation in one year is σ, then the standard deviation deviation in k years will be the square root of k times σ. This property of random variates has been demonstrated for log differences in stock prices, earnings, and interest rates.

The expected mean of a lognormal variate is given by Aitchison and Brown [1957]:

$$E \, avg \, exp(u) = exp(avg(u) + \sigma^2/2)$$

If the expected change in the natural logarithms of prices is zero:

$$E \, avg \, u_t = 0$$

Then, the expected change in the antilog is:

$$E \text{ avg } \exp(u) = \exp(\sigma^2/2) \tag{5}$$

The variance of $\exp(u)$ is given by:

$E \sigma^2 \exp(u) = \exp(4\sigma^2/2)$

The probability density function is given by:

$Y = (1/\sqrt{2\pi})\exp^{-5(u-\mu)/115}$

where σ is the cross-sectional standard deviation, i.e., the standard deviation across firms.

APPENDIX VIII

Notes to Chapters

Chapter 1 Overview

Strictly speaking, one doesn't predict probabilities: one estimates probabilities from relative frequencies of occurrence in the past. One assumes stationarity (time independence of probabilities), and hence that the same probabilities hold for the future. This is frequently not the case. The size of the probability and the circumstances under which you use it can make a big difference. If the probability of rain (or a deficit) is 40%, but you estimate 30%, that's not a big difference practically speaking. In other circumstances (death, accidents, disease, default on debt, failure of a part) this difference (in insurance rates, or risk aversion) between a 1% and a 5% or 10% probability of occurrence can make a great deal of difference. Witness the experience of banks with loans.

Chapter 2 The Standard Deviation, the Normal Distribution and Natural Logarithms—Concepts Useful to Studying the Stock Market

The log normal distribution is discussed more fully in Chapter 3.

Chapter 3 The Statistical Basis for Estimating Future Probable Changes in Stock Prices

A detailed description of the log-normal distribution of stock prices may be found in M.F.M. Osborne, "Brownian Motion in the Stock Market," *Operations Research*, vol. 7, pp. 145–73. Other financial variables, such as corporate earnings and interest rates, have the same statistical characteristics. See notes to Chapter 5.

Chapter 4 How Knowing the Probability Can Improve Your Investment Decisions

The illustrations is this chapter are fictional, though they are based on real life examples.

Illustrations of the use of probability for investment decisions are given in

Murphy, J.E., *With Interest: How to Profit from Interest Rate Fluctuations*, 1986, Dow Jones–Irwin, Homewood, Illinois.

Chapter 5 The Dispersion of Stock Prices

I measure dispersion by the standard deviation of changes in the logarithms of prices.

The assumption that transactions take place evenly in time is not true. Volume is much higher today than it was a decade or two ago. Yet the square root rule does describe the relationship approximately. The stationarity of the standard deviation is discussed in Chapter 9.

The terminology on the "square root of time rule" is the following. If we compute differences in the logs of a price series, the standard deviation of those log price changes rises with the square root of the differencing interval. I also call that differencing interval "time" and "holding period." In the terminology of a random walk, it is called the "step length." In the terminology of fluctuations of coin tossing, its the number of flips of the coin. All these terms designate the same general phenomena.

That the rule characterizes random walks, or random variables, is well-known and can be found in books on statistics and articles on Brownian Motion.

The evidence for the rule in the stock market is given in Osborne, M.F.M., "Brownian Motion in the Stock Market," *Operations Research*, vol. 7, 1959, pp. 145–73. Evidence for the rule in earnings appears in Osborne, M.F.M. and Murphy, J.E., "Financial Analogs of Physical Brownian Motion, as Illustrated by Earnings," *The Financial Review*, vol. 19, no. 2, 1984, pp. 153–72.

The formula for computing the difference in the logs of price is:

$$x(k) = \log_e \left(p(t+k)/p(t) \right)$$

or equivalently

$$x(k) = \log_e p(t+k) - \log_e p(t)$$

In this formula k is the differencing interval, or time. The standard deviation of $x(k)$ rises with the square root of k, or with k^5. The variable $x(k)$ is also the percent change in p (or price) between times t and t+k, using continuous compounding.

In Table 5.2 the mean and median is not included.

Chapter 6   The Basic Model of the Stock Market

I believe that Osborne was the first person to propose the model described here based on a log-normal distribution; others have since put forth similar models. Osborne examined the relationship between what he called the differencing interval and the standard deviation, $s(t)=s(0)x\ t^5$; he used that relationship to demonstrate Brownian Motion in the market. He also pointed out that the log-normal distribution of changes in prices would result in an annual increase in the market of about 5% per year. Surprisingly, this important characteristic is seldom recognized in the literature, despite the fact that it is largely responsible for the market's long-term growth. *[handwritten: inflation ?]*

The nature of the distribution of changes in stock prices has been the result *[handwritten: economic growth]* of considerable study and debate; but there is no question that the distribution is approximately normal. The Student or t distribution approximates the normal for large n. Praetz argues that the Student t distribution is a better approximation of stock prices; Mandelbrot reports that monthly prices are stable Paretian while the averages seem to be normal. It should be noted that the sums of random variables approach the normal with increasing time. For other work on the subject see the following:

Blattberg, Robert C. and Gonedes, Nicholas J., "A Comparison of the Stable and Student Distributions as Statistical Models for Stock Prices," *Journal of Business* 47 (April 1974), 244–80.

Blattberg, Robert C. and Gonedes, Nicholas J., "A Comparison of the Stable and Student Distributions as Statistical Models for Stock Prices: Reply," *Journal of Business*, 50 (Jan. 1977), 78–79.

Mandelbrot, B., "The Variation of Certain Speculative Prices," *Journal of Business*, 36 (Oct, 1963), 394–419.

Mandelbrot, B., "The Variation of Some Other Speculative Prices," *Journal of Business*, 40 (Oct. 1967), 393–413.

Mandelbrot, B. and Fama, E. F., "The Behavior of Stock Market Prices," *Journal of Business*, 38 (Jan. 1965), 34–105.

Mandelbrot, B. and Taylor, H. M., "On the Distribution of Stock Price Differences," *Operations Research*, 15 (1967), 1057–62

Osborne, M.F.M., "Brownian Motion in the Stock Market," *Operations Research*, vol. 7, 1959, pp. 145–73.

Osborne, M.F.M., *The Stock Market and Finance from a Physicist's Viewpoint*, published by the author (1977), 3803 24th Avenue, Temple Hills, MD, 20748.

Praetz, Peter D., "The Distribution of Share Price Changes," *Journal of Business*, 45 (Jan. 1972), 49–55.

Praetz, Peter D., "A Comparison of the Stable and Student Distributions as Statistical Models for Stock Prices: Comment," *Journal of Business*, 50 (Jan. 1977), 76–77.

Chapter 8 How to Reduce Common Stock Portfolio Risk
The literature on this topic is very extensive, particularly theoretical articles. Latane describes the theoretical model for the effect of the number of securities on non-market risk and shows how the model applies to the Fisher Lorie data. Other writers have reached similar conclusions. Latane, Henry A., "Cross-Section Regularities in Returns in Investments in Common Stocks," *Journal of Business*, 46 (Oct. 1973), 512–17.

Blume, Marshall E., "On the Assessment of Risk," *Journal of Finance*, 27 (Mar. 1971), 1–10.

Brennan, Michael J., "The Optimal Number of Securities in a Risky Asset Portfolio When There are Fixed Costs of Transaction: Theory and Some Empirical Results," *Journal of Financial and Quantitative Analysis*, 10 (Sept. 1975), 483–96.

Elton, Edwin J. and Gruber, Martin, J., "Risk Reduction and Portfolio Size: An Analytical Solution," *Journal of Business*, 50 (Oct. 1977), 415–37.

Evans, John L. and Archer, Stephen H., "Diversification and the Reduction of Dispersion: An Empirical Analysis," *Journal of Finance*, 23 (Dec. 1966), 761–67.

Jennings, Edward, "An Empirical Analysis of Some Aspects of Common Stock Diversification," *Journal of Financial and Quantitative Analysis*, 6 (Mar. 1971), 797–813.

Johnson, A. and B. Shannon, "A Note on the Diversification and Reduction of Risk," *Journal of Financial Economics*, 1 (1974), 365–72.

Latane, Henry A., "Cross-Section Regularities in Returns in Investments in Common Stocks," *Journal of Business*, 46 (Oct. 1973), 512–17.

Markowitz, Harry, *Portfolio Selection*, New York, Wiley, 1959.

Markowitz, Harry, "Markowitz Revisited," *Financial Analysts Journal*, 32 (Sept.–Oct. 1976), 47–52.

Wagner, W. and Lau, S., "The Effect of Diversification on Risk," *Financial Analysts Journal*, 27 (Nov.–Dec. 1971), 48–53.

Whitmore, G. A., "Diversification and the Reduction of Dispersion: A Note," *Journal of Financial and Quantitative Analysis*, 5 (June 1970), 263–64.

Chapter 9 Are There Changes in Stock Market Volatility?
R.R. Officer demonstrated in 1973 that the stock market over the period 1897–1926 was not stationary; it was much more volatile at the time of the Great Depression than in prior or subsequent periods. Officer used a running 12-month standard deviation of monthly returns, though the precise definition of how he computed the returns is not clear.

Boness, A. A. Chen and S. Jatusipitak, "Investigation of Nonstationarity in Prices," *Journal of Business*, 47 (Oct. 1974), 518–37.

Officer, R.R., "The Variability of the Market Factor of the New York Stock Exchange," *Journal of Business*, 46 (July 1973), 434–53

Chapter 10 Predicting Probable Returns from a Single Stock
The estimated probability distribution of returns excludes both the dividend and an estimate of the mean change. The probability distribution can be adjusted to include these elements.

Chapter 11 Predicting Probable Returns on a Mutual Fund
It would be better to calculate the standard deviation using the change in logarithms of prices. In calculating probable returns, I've ignored the 6.8% mean increase in price. Whether this should be set at zero (as I've done) or not is a matter of debate.

Sharp, William F., "Mutual Fund Performance," *Journal of Business*, 39 (Jan. 1966), 119–38.

Chapter 12 Predicting the Probability of Loss
Murphy, J.E. and Osborne, M.F.M., "Games of Chance and the Probability of Corporate Profit or Loss," *Financial Management*, Vol. 8, No.2. Summer 1979, 82–88.

Chapter 13 Predicting Probable Changes in Earnings
The distribution of changes in earnings of individual corporations is approximately log-normal with a standard deviation that increases approximately with the square root of time.

Chapter 14 Predicting Probable Changes in Profit Margins
Although the example is fictional, the practice of anticipating an improvement in considering or making acquisitions is common.

Chapter 15 How to Estimate the Average Future Return from Stocks
Osborne, M.F.M., "Brownian Motion in the Stock Market," *Operations Research*, vol. 7, 1959, pp. 145–73.

Chapter 16 The Law of the Distribution of Wealth
Fisher, Lawrence and Lorie, James H., "Some Studies of Variability of Returns on Investments in Common Stocks," *Journal of Business*, 43 (April 1970), 99–134.

Chapter 17 Diversification Across Time
This chapter was suggested by Dick Jensen of First Asset Management, Minneapolis.

Chapter 18 Predicting Dividend Changes
Murphy, J.E. & Johnson, R.S. Predicting, "Dividend Changes," *Trusts & Estates*, August 1972, 638–41.

Chapter 19 Basis for Predicting the Probability of Loss
In view of the high correlation between negative income (or deficits) and bankruptcy, the statistical properties of changes in earnings, and the ability to project the probability distribution of those changes, it is more useful, I believe, to use the conceptual framework of this chapter for forecasting the probability of bankruptcy, or discontinuance. We found that the probability of loss correlated very well with the incidence of bankruptcy on both an *ex anti* and *ex post* basis. I think this is perferable to use of ratios or discriminant analysis.

Murphy, J.E. and Osborne, M.F.M., "Games of Chance and the Probability of Corporate Profit or Loss," *Financial Management*, Vol. 8, No.2. Summer 1979. 82–88.

Osborne, M.F.M. and Murphy, J.E., "Financial Analogs of Physical Brownian Motion, as Illustrated by Earnings," *The Financial Review*, vol. 19, no. 2, 1984, pp. 153–72.

Chapter 20   The First Five Laws of Finance
The First Law follows from a natural property of the random walk. If the steps (the first differences in the logs) are independent, or nearly independent (i.e., small or zero correlation), the successive positions themselves (the sum of the steps) are highly correlated (Second Law). See Osborne, M.F.M., *The Stock Market and Finance from a Physicist's Viewpoint*, (1977), published by the author, 3803 24th Avenue, Temple Hills, MD, 20748, Vol. II, p. 477.

Murphy, J.E. and Nelson, J.R. "A Note on the Stability of P/E Ratios," *Financial Analysts Journal*, March–April 1969, pp. 77–80.

Murphy, J.E. and Nelson, J.R. "Random and Nonrandom Relationships Among Financial Variables: a Financial Model," *Journal of Financial and Quantitative Analysis*, March 1971, Vol VI, No. 2, pp. 875–85.

Murphy, J.E. and Nelson, J.R., "Five Principles of Financial Relationships," *Financial Analysts Journal*, March–April 1971, Vol. 27, No. 2, pp. 38–52.

Murphy, J.E. and Nelson, J.R., "Five New Financial Principles: Reply to a Comment," *Financial Analysts Journal*, March–April 1972, Vol. 28, No. 2., p. 112.

APPENDIX IX

Bibliography

Notes on Bibliography

One of the best articles on the stock market is Osborne's "Brownian Motion in the Stock Market." Though technical, it lays out the underlying character of the market and shows the effect of the holding period (time) on dispersion. Osborne's article, and a number of others may be found in Cootner's *The Random Character of the Stock Market*. Richard Brealey's *An Introduction to Risk and Return from Common Stocks* and *Security Prices in a Competitive Market* provide good overviews of the subject and, unlike Cootner, are not technical.

Probably the best treatment of randomness in earnings is Rayner and Little's *Higgedly, Piggedly Growth Again*, though it deals with British data. The other principal articles—there aren't very many—are listed in the bibliography. Apart from the studies by Russell Nelson and me, there is little work on randomness in other financial variables. Both subjects deserve more study, preferably along the lines of Osborne's "Brownian Motion." Brealey covers randomness in earnings.

I am not aware that others have classified variables or drawn inferences from that classification in the way done here.

One of the best studies of the cross-sectional behavior of stock prices is Fisher and Lorie's "Some Studies of Variability of Returns on Investments in Common Stocks" which appeared in the *Journal of Business* in 1970. Although the article is entirely descriptive, an excellent theoretical analysis and summary was given by Latane in a 1973 issue of the same journal; it is called "Cross-Section Regularities in Returns in Investments in Common Stocks."

There are many studies on the return on the market over time, nearly all descriptive, few analytic.

There are even more studies on reducing portfolio risk, most of them theoretical, some descriptive, mainly on the beta controversy. Markowitz's *Portfolio Selection* is classic and is probably the best. It is standard statistics, except for the discussion of the "efficient frontier." That concept is difficult

211

to apply because the inputs are unknowable, though this weakness does not seem to have diminished the popularity of the topic.

Many valuable empirical analyses of credit problems have been done, usually under the topic of predicting bankruptcy. Prominent is the work of Altman and Beaver. Nearly all of this work has an unnecessary weakness: the variables from which the predictive formulas are derived are not dimensionless, though they could be. Altman, for example, uses sales in calculating his equations. The use of sales makes the result particular and arbitrary. It would have been preferable to divide variables by their standard deviation and thereby achieve a generality that crossed industry lines and permits application of probability theory to the issue. The result would be a different and, I think, more useful perspective.

The prediction of loss in this book—the same underlying problem as bankruptcy—uses a dimensionless variable; this permits putting the analysis in terms of probability and deriving an analytical tool that is independent of industry. See Murphy and Osborne, "Predicting the Probability of Loss." The probability chapters in this book illustrate how that can be done. The other literature on this approach is limited.

The other references that I found particularly useful are mentioned in the text. In general, the work that was most helpful to me came not from students of finance, but from outsiders like Feller, Mandelbrot (*Fractals*), and Osborne, who looked at the data from a slightly different perspective, who viewed it in more general terms, and tried to apply probability to the subject matter.

Aitchison, J. and J.A.C. Brown, *The Lognormal Distribution with Special Reference to its Uses in Economics*, Cambridge University Press, London, 1981.

Alexander, G. and J.C. Francis, *Portfolio Analysis*, Prentice-Hall, 1986.

Barnes, A. and D. Downes, "A Reexamination of the Empirical Distribution of Stock Price Changes," *Journal of the American Statistical Association*, 68 (June 1973) 348–50.

Beaver, William H., "Financial Ratios as Predictions of Failure," *Empirical Research in Accounting: Selected Studies*, 1966, Supplement to Vol. 4, *Journal of Accounting Research*, 62–87.

Beaver, William H., "The Time Series Behavior of Earnings," *Empirical Research in Accounting: Selected Studies*, 1970, Supplement to Vol. 8, *Journal of Accounting Research*, 62–87.

Black, F. and M. Scholes, "The Effects of Dividend Yield and Dividend Policy on Common Stock Prices and Returns," *Journal of Financial Economics*, 1 (May 1974), 1–22.

Blattberg, Robert C. and Gonedes, Nicholas J., "A Comparison of the Stable and Student Distributions as Statistical Models for Stock Prices," *Journal of Business*, 47 (April 1974), 244–80.

Blattberg, Robert C. and Gonedes, Nicholas J., "A Comparison of the Stable and Student Distributions as Statistical Models for Stock Prices: Reply," *Journal of Business*, 50 (January 1977), 78–79.

Blume, Marshall E., "On the Assessment of Risk," *Journal of Finance*, 27 (March 1971), 1–10.

Boness, A. A. Chen and S. Jatusipitak, "Investigation of Nonstationarity in Prices," *Journal of Business*, 47 (October 1974), 518–37.

Brealey, Richard A., *An Introduction to Risk and Return from Common Stocks*, M.I.T. Press, 1969.

Brealey, Richard A., *Security Prices in a Competitive Market,* MIT Press, Cambridge,1971.

Brealey, Richard A., "The Distribution and Independence of Successive Rates of Return in the U.S. Equity Markets," *Journal of Business Finance*, Summer 1970.

Brennan, Michael J., "The Optimal Number of Securities in a Risky Asset Portfolio When There are Fixed Costs of Transactions: Theory and Some Empirical Results," *Journal of Financial and Quantitative Analysis*, 10 (September 1975), 483–96.

Brigham, Eugene F. and Pappas, James L., "Duration of Growth, Changes in Growth Rates, and Corporate Share Prices," *Financial Analysts Journal* (May–June 1966), 157–61.

Brigham, Eugene F. and Pappas, James L., "Rates of Return on Common Stocks," *Journal of Business*, 41 (July 1969), 302–30.

Brooks, Leroy D. and D. A. Buckmaster, "Further Evidence of the Time Series Properties of Accounting Income," *Journal of Finance* (December 1977) 1359–72.

Campanella, F. B. *The Measurement of Portfolio Risk Exposure*, Lexington Books, Lexington, Mass., 1972.

Cohn, Timothy A., "Adjusted Maximum Likelihood Estimation of the Moments of Lognormal Populations from Type I Censored Samples," U.S. Geological Survey, Reston, VA 1987.

Cooley, Philip L, Rodney L. Roenfeldt and Naval K. Modanni, "Interdependence of Market Risk Measures," *Journal of Business*, 50 (July 1977), 356–63.

Cootner, P. H., Ed., *The Random Character of Stock Prices*, M.I.T. Press, Cambridge, 1964.

Elton, Edwin J. and Gruber, Martin, J., "Risk Reduction and Portfolio Size: An Analytical Solution," *Journal of Business*, 50 (October 1977), 415–37.

Evans, John L. and Archer, Stephen H., "Diversification and the Reduction of Dispersion: An Empirical Analysis," *Journal of Finance*, 23 (December 1966), 761–67.

Fama, E.F., "Random Walks in Stock Market Prices," *Financial Analysts Journal* (Sept.–Oct. 1965), 55–58.

Fama, Eugene F., "The Behavior of Stock Market Prices," *Journal of Business*, 38 (January 1965), 45–46.

Feller, W., *An Introduction to Probability Theory and Its Applications*, Vol. I, Wiley, N.Y., 2nd ed., 1957, 344.

Fisher, L., "Outcomes for 'Random' Investment in Common Stocks Listed on the New York Stock Exchange," *Journal of Business*, 38 (April 1965), 149–61.

Fisher, James and Lorie, Lawrence, *A Half Century of Returns on Stocks and Bonds*, University of Chicago, 1977.

Fisher, Lawrence and Lorie, James H., "Some Studies of Variability of Returns on Investments in Common Stocks," *Journal of Business*, 43 (April 1970), 99–134.

Flavin, Marjorie A., "Excess Volatility in the Financial Markets: A Reassessment of the Empirical Evidence," *Journal of Political Economy*, 91 (December 1983), 929–56.

Fleming, Robert M., "How Risky is the Market?," *Journal of Business*, 46 (July 1973), 404–24.

Friend, Irwin and Vickers, Douglas, "Portfolio Selection and Investment Performance," *Journal of Finance*, 20 (September 1965), 391–415.

Fogler, H. Russell, *Analyzing the Stock Market: A Quantitative Approach*, Grid, Inc., Columbus, Ohio, 1973.

Garman, M. B. and M. J. Klass, "On the Estimation of Security Price Volatilities from Historical Data," *Journal of Business*, 53 (January 1980), 67–78.

Ibbotson, Roger G. and Sinquefield, Rex A., "Stocks, Bonds, Bills, and Inflation: Year-by-Year Historical Returns (1926–1974)," *Journal of Business*, 49 (January 1976), 11–47.

Jennings, Edward, "An Empirical Analysis of Some Aspects of Common Stock Diversification," *Journal of Financial and Quantitative Analysis*, 6 (March 1971), 797–813.

Johnson, A. and B. Shannon, "A Note on the Diversification and Reduction of Risk," *Journal of Financial Economics*, 1 (1974), 365–72.

King, Benjamin F., "Market and Industry Factors in Stock Price Behavior," *Journal of Business*, 39 (January 1966), 139–90.

Latane, Henry A., "Cross-Section Regularities in Returns in Investments in Common Stocks," *Journal of Business*, 46 (October 1973), 512–17.

Lewis, Alan L., Sheen T. Kassdout, R. Dennis Brehm, and Jack Johnston, "The Ibbotson-Sinquefield Simulation Made Easy," *Journal of Business*, 53 (April 1980), 205–14.

Lintner, John, "Security Prices, Risk, and Maximal Gains from Diversification," *Journal of Finance*, December 1965.

Lintner, John, "Distribution of Incomes of Corporations among Dividends, Retained Earnings and Taxes," *American Economic Review* (May 1956), 97–113.

Lintner, John and Robert Glauber, "Higgledy Piggledy Growth in America?" Seminar on the Analysis of Security Prices, Center for Research in Security Prices, Graduate School of Business, The University of Chicago, May 11–12, 1967.

Lorie, James H. and Hamilton, Mary T., *The Stock Market: Theories and Evidence*, Richard D. Irwin, Homewood, Illinois, 1973.

Lorie, James H., "Some Comments on Recent Quantitative and Formal Research on the Stock Market," *Journal of Business*, 39 (January 1966), 107–109.

Maginn, John L. and Tuttle, Donald L. editors, *Managing Investment Portfolios: A Dynamic Process*, Warren, Gorham & Lamont, Boston, 1983.

Mains, Norman E., "Risk, the Pricing of Capital Assets, and the Evaluation of Investment Portfolios: Comment," *Journal of Business*, 50 (July 1977), 371–84.

Mandelbrot, B., *Fractals*, W.H. Freeman, San Francisco, 1977.

Mandelbrot, B., "The Variation of Certain Speculative Prices," *Journal of Business*, 36 (October 1963), 394–419.

Mandelbrot, Benoit, "Forecasts of Future Prices, Unbiased Markets, and 'Martingale' Models," *Journal of Business*, 39 (January 1966), 242–55.

Mandelbrot, B. and Fama, E. F., "The Behavior of Stock Market Prices," *Journal of Business*, 38 (January 1965), 34–105.

Mandelbrot, B. and Taylor, H. M., "On the Distribution of Stock Price Differences," *Operations Research*, 15 (1967), 1057–62.

Markowitz, Harry, *Portfolio Selection*, New York, Wiley, 1959.

Markowitz, Harry, "Markowitz Revisited," *Financial Analysts Journal*, 32 (September–October 1976), 47–52.

Miller, M. and F. Modigliani, "Dividend Policy, Growth, and the Valuation of Shares," *Journal of Business* (October 1961), 411–33.

Murphy, J.E., *With Interest*, Dow Jones-Irwin, Homewood, Illinois, 1987.

Murphy, J.E., "Relative Growth of Earnings. Per Share—Past and Future," *Financial Analysts Journal* (November–December 1966), 73–76.

Murphy, J.E., "Return on Equity Capital, Dividend Payout and Growth of Earnings Per Share," *Financial Analysts Journal* (May–June 1967), 91–93.

Murphy, J.E., "Earnings Growth and Price Change in the Same Time Period," *Financial Analysts Journal* (January–February 1968), 97–99.

Murphy, J.E., "Effect of Leverage on Profitability, Growth and Market Valuation of Common Stock," *Financial Analysts Journal* (July–August 1968), 121–23.

Murphy, J.E. and Johnson, R.S., "Predicting Dividend Changes," *Trusts & Estates* (August 1972), 638–41.

Murphy, J.E. and Nelson, J.R. "A Note on the Stability of P/E Ratios," *Financial Analysts Journal* (March–April 1969), 77–80.

Murphy, J.E. and Nelson, J.R. "Random and Nonrandom Relationships Among Financial Variables: a Financial Model," *Journal of Financial and Quantitative Analysis*, Vol VI, No. 2 (March 1971), 875–85.

Murphy, J.E. and Nelson, J.R., "Five Principles of Financial Relationships," *Financial Analysts Journal*, Vol. 27, No. 2 (March–April 1971), 38–52. (Reprinted in The Institute of Chartered Financial Analysts, *Supplementary Readings in Financial Analysis*: 1972. 1971. R.D. Irwin, Homewood, Illinois, 208–22.

Murphy, J.E. and J. R. Nelson,, "Five New Financial Principles: Reply to a Comment," *Financial Analysts Journal*, Vol. 28, No. 2 (March–April 1972), 112.

Murphy, J.E. and Osborne, M.F.M., "Games of Chance and the Probability of Corporate Profit or Loss," *Financial Management*, Vol. 8, No. 2 (Summer 1979), 82–88.

Murphy, J.E., and Osborne, M.F.M., "Predicting the Volatility of Interest Rates," *Journal of Portfolio Management*, (Winter 1985), pp. 66–69.

Murphy, J.E. and Stevenson, H.W., "Price/Earnings Ratios and Future Growth of Earnings and Dividends," *Financial Analysts Journal*, Vol. 23, No. 6 (November–December 1967), 111–14.

Nicholson, S. F., "Price–Earnings Ratios," *Financial Analysts Journal* (July–August) 1960, 43–46.

Niederhoffer, Victor and P. J. Regan, "Earnings Changes, Analysts' Forecasts and Stock Prices," *Financial Analysts Journal*, 1982, 65–71.

Officer, R.R., "The Variability of the Market Factor of the New York Stock Exchange," *Journal of Business*, 46 (July 1973), 434–53.

Officer, R.R., "The Distribution of Stock Returns," *The Journal of the American Statistical Association*, 67 (December 1972), 807–12.

Osborne, M.F.M., "Brownian Motion in the Stock Market," *Operations Research*, vol. 7, 1959, pp. 145–73. (Also in Cootner.)

Osborne, M.F.M., *The Stock Market and Finance from a Physicist's Viewpoint* (1977), published by the author, 3803 24th Avenue, Temple Hills, MD 20748.

Osborne, M.F.M. and Murphy, J.E., "Brownian Motion of Corporate Earnings in a Varying Probability Field," Fall 1980 Seminar, Institute for Quantitative Research in Finance. Available from the Institute, Columbia University, New York, N.Y.

Osborne, M.F.M. and Murphy, J.E., "Financial Analogs of Physical Brownian Motion, as Illustrated by Earnings," *The Financial Review*, Vol. 19, no. 2, 1984, 153–72.

Osborne, M.F.M. and Murphy, J.E., "Brownian Motion in the Interest Rate Considered as the Price of Money," Eastern Finance Association, Annual Meeting, April 20–23, 1983. New York, N.Y.

Parkinson, Michael, "The Extreme Value Method for Estimating the Variance of the Rate of Return," *Journal of Business*, 53 (January 1980), 61–66.

Price, Lee N., "Choosing Between Growth and Yield," *Financial Analysts Journal* (July–August 1979).

Praetz, Peter D., "The Distribution of Share Price Changes," *Journal of Business*, 45 (January 1972), 49–55.

Praetz, Peter D., "A Comparison of the Stable and Student Distributions as Statistical Models for Stock Prices: Comment," *Journal of Business*, 50 (January 1977), 76–77.

Rayner, A.C. and I.M.D. Little, *Higgledy Piggledy Growth Again*, Basil Blackwell, Oxford, 1966.

Rothstein, Marvin, "On Geometric and Arithmetic Portfolio Performance Indexes," *Journal of Financial and Quantitative Analysis*, 7 (September 1972), 1983–92.

Sharp, W.F., "Risk Aversion in the Stock Market: Some Empirical Evidence," *Journal of Finance*, 20 (September 1965), 416–22.

Sharp, William F., "Mutual Fund Performance," *Journal of Business*, 39 (January 1966), 119–38.

Scott, M.F.G., "Relative Share Prices and Yields," *Oxford Economic Papers* (October 1962), 218–50.

Teichmoeller, J., "Distribution of Stock Price Changes," *Journal of the American Statistical Association*, 66 (June 1971), 282–84.

Wagner, W. and Lau, S., "The Effect of Diversification on Risk," *Financial Analysts Journal*, 27 (November–December 1971), 48–53.

Whitmore, G. A., "Diversification and the Reduction of Dispersion: A Note," *Journal of Financial and Quantitative Analysis*, 5 (June 1970), 263–64.

Young, W. E. and R. H. Trent, "Geometric Mean Approximations of Individual Security and Portfolio Performance," *Journal of Financial and Quantitative Analysis*, 4 (June 1969), 179–200.

Index